Needlepoint
on Plastic Canvas

Needlepoint on Plastic Canvas

ELISABETH BRENNER DE NITTO

CHARLES SCRIBNER'S SONS · NEW YORK

Library of Congress Cataloging in Publication Data
De Nitto, Elisabeth Brenner.
  Needlepoint on plastic canvas.
  1. Canvas embroidery. I. Title. II. Title:
Plastic canvas.
TT778.C3D46   746.4′4   78-705
ISBN 0-684-15534-6
ISBN 0-684-15577-X pbk.

1 3 5 7 9 11 13 15 17 19 M/C 20 18 16 14 12 10 8 6 4 2
1 3 5 7 9 11 13 15 17 19 M/P 20 18 16 14 12 10 8 6 4 2

COLOR PRINTED IN JAPAN
TEXT AND BLACK AND WHITE ILLUSTRATIONS PRINTED IN THE UNITED STATES OF AMERICA

To my mother,

Josefine Brenner,

*who, not always with objective justification,
has had confidence in my abilities and
has never hesitated to contribute
her time and effort to helping me*

ACKNOWLEDGMENTS

I must also acknowledge the contributions of the other members of my family. My particular gratitude to my husband, Dennis, for encouraging me and, on a more practical level, with a minimum of complaint, for taking time from his own writing to advise me on problems of style and approach.

My older son, Daryl, not only took some of the photographs that appear in this book but also good-naturedly accepted the situation of a mother who spent hours of each day stitching or drawing.

A special thanks to my younger son, Devin —for just being there as a source and recipient of unqualified love.

Others also deserve credit: Dan P. Du Vall and David T. Stevenson of E. I. Du Pont de Nemours & Co., and Stephanie Schuss of Columbia-Minerva, who encouraged me through their enthusiasm and generous supplies of canvas; Patricia Feeney, who assisted me in inking in the graphs; and my editor, Elinor Parker, who had confidence in the book and patience with its author.

CONTENTS

Introduction   9

1. MATERIALS AND SUPPLIES   *11*

2. HOME ACCESSORIES   *17*

    Welcome Picture   *19*

    Tree Wall Hanging   *23*

    Picture Frames   *27*

    Mirror Frame   *38*

    Tissue Box Cover   *41*

    Butterfly Place Mat   *44*

    Butterfly Napkin Ring   *47*

    Flower Coasters   *49*

    Vexar (Free-Form) Rug   *51*

    Geometric Rug   *54*

3. DESK ACCESSORIES   *57*

    Typewriter Cover   *59*

    Desk Pad   *62*

    Stamp Box   *64*

    Checkbook Cover   *66*

4. PERSONAL ACCESSORIES   69

    Clutch Bag   71

    Eyeglasses Case   74

    Key Holder   76

    Belt   77

    Carrying Bag   79

    Wall Organizer   82

    Sewing or Storage Box   87

    Scissors Case   90

    Pincushion   92

    Trinket Box   94

5. GIFTS TO GIVE OR KEEP   95

    Potted Flowers   97

    Lizzy (Stand-up) Doll   103

    Photo Album Cover   106

    Straw Basket   109

    Alphabet Letters   111

    Embroidered Alphabet Sculptures   115

6. GLOSSARY OF STITCHES AND
   FINISHING TECHNIQUES   117

    List of Suppliers   127

INTRODUCTION

This book has several characteristics, I believe, that distinguish it from the numerous volumes on needlepoint which appear in bookstores each year. There is one, however, that goes beyond the author's skill, imagination, or dedication: this book is the first in which all the projects make use of plastic mesh canvas, a new product that has recently appeared on the market. For readers to appreciate the significance of this technological breakthrough for craftspersons in the field of needlepoint requires a reminder on my part of the traditional method of working on a needlepoint project.

As anyone familiar with needlepoint is aware, most stitching is presently done on fabric canvas. There are many disadvantages in using this type of material. First, fabric canvas usually pulls out of shape. This is why the tedious process of blocking becomes an essential part of any needlepoint project done on fabric canvas. Even the most careful blocking often leaves the end product with a certain ill-fitting appearance that precludes a professional look. Furthermore, canvas edges fray, and there is often a good deal of waste because of the necessity of hemming to hide frayed edges.

Plastic mesh canvas solves each of these problems, and, in addition, has outstanding advantages of its own. There is no need for blocking: plastic mesh canvas does not pull out of shape while being worked on. It can be cut to any shape, does not fray, and requires no hemming; so there is no need to make the usual seam allowances. The finished product is the size to which the canvas was cut.

These advantages would in themselves make plastic mesh canvas a marvelous material, but there is also a unique quality that allows a wide range of new ideas. Three-dimensional objects that could be made with fabric canvas only with the greatest difficulty are finally possible. A box, for example, requires laborious starching and additional stiffening with lining if made on fabric canvas, whereas with plastic mesh canvas it needs only to be cut, embroidered, and assembled.

All of the projects in this book are either easier to create with plastic mesh canvas rather than fabric canvas or would be impossible by the older means without frustrating hours of blocking. I have found that working with plastic canvas has stimulated my imagination by offering new dimensions in needlecraft, and I hope my readers will also be excited as they work on these projects and go beyond them.

I have attempted to organize this volume and to choose projects so that any person, regardless of his or her previous experience in needlepoint, will have no difficulty in following my directions. I have organized the book into three major parts. The first part is devoted to "Materials and Supplies." This chapter explains the characteristics of plastic canvas and the types presently available. There are recommendations on how to work with the material, such as cutting, transferring a design, and finishing a project, as well as comments on yarns and equipment. I believe that beginners in particular should read this chapter with care.

The major part of this volume is devoted to the projects themselves and is divided into four sections: Home Accessories, Desk Accessories, Personal Accessories, and Gifts to Give or Keep. For each project there are clear and concise instructions, illustrated with photographs, and a detailed graph of each design.

The third part, Chapter 6, is a glossary of the stitches used in embroidering the projects.

My main goal in creating each project was to combine usefulness with imaginative design. In addition, I have attempted to include items that range from the simple to the more sophisticated, although none of them requires a great deal of previous experience to be carried out (some of the projects, such as the straw basket, could even be made by children). I have also attempted, however, to satisfy the needs of embroiderers who have achieved a certain degree of expertise.

This book will have completely fulfilled its purpose if it not only gives embroiderers pleasure in making the projects and satisfaction in the final products, but also inspires them to design their own works based on new dimensions in needlepoint.

·1·

MATERIALS AND SUPPLIES

Figure 1

Figure 2

In this chapter are succinctly indicated all the procedures, approaches, and equipment you will need to complete the projects successfully. The main subjects are the following: canvas, yarns, transferring designs to canvas, finishing, embroidery hints, and equipment. I recommend that you read these pages carefully before beginning work on any project.

CANVAS

There are two types of plastic canvas presently available:

"Fashion Ease" is a 7-mesh canvas. It is most often sold in a sheet size of approximately 11 inches by 14 inches. Other sizes are available, such as small squares and various other shapes.

"Vexar"® is manufactured by Du Pont. This canvas can be obtained in 10-mesh and 5-mesh. The latter is particularly suitable for rugs or other projects on which larger stitches are used. One of the advantages of Vexar is that it is produced as yard goods. You are therefore not limited in the choice of projects by the size of the canvas available as in the case of Fashion Ease. Keep in mind that some stores sell Vexar by the yard; others limit themselves to various precut sheet sizes.

The canvas must be cut with care. In most instances it is easier to embroider a piece before cutting it out (see Figure 1). It is very important, however, to leave one row (or ridge) all around in order to be able to finish the edges of the embroidery (see Figure 2).

YARNS

Persian Yarn: Most projects in this book have been embroidered with Persian yarn (manufactured by Paternayan). It is of excellent quality and is available in a color range of over three hundred shades. Other yarn of similar quality can be used. Where doubled Persian yarn is indicated, a heavier embroidery yarn can be substituted. In that case, the yardage required will then be half the amount indicated.

Rug Yarn: The Vexar rug is worked with Pat-Rug yarn, also from Paternayan, which is of excellent quality. If you purchase another brand, do choose one that will give maximum durability and will not fade.

The choice of yarn colors is, of course, personal; those indicated are meant only as suggestions. Use your own preferences—perhaps colors that best fit into your decor or match your wardrobe.

TRANSFERRING THE DESIGNS TO CANVAS

The detailed graph of each design enables you to count the stitches as they are being worked on the canvas. There are basically two methods, however, for transferring the outline of the design onto the canvas. If the project is executed in continental stitch, it is easiest first to outline the design with a row of continental stitches. The second approach is to use a permanent marker (Nepo Needlework Markers are particularly suitable). It is a good idea to choose a marker color close to the yarn color just in case any ink rubs off. Apply the marker sparingly because the plastic canvas does not absorb color.

FINISHING

As mentioned in the introduction, no hemming or seam allowance is needed for plastic canvas. However, the edges all around require finishing, and a binding or overcast stitch is most suitable. When two edges of canvas are to be joined, simply hold them together, treating them as one layer, and bind stitch or overcast.

EMBROIDERY HINTS

It is the rigidity of the canvas that enables the user to create these marvelous three-dimensional projects. On the other hand, this rigidity requires that a stitch be completed in two steps because the canvas does not bend sufficiently for the needle to be pulled down and up in one motion.

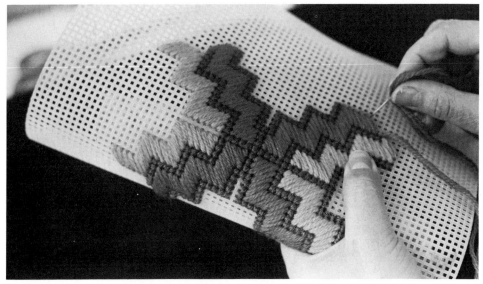

Figure 3

Step 1: push the needle down, pull the yarn through all the way.

Step 2: push the needle up in the desired hole, pull yarn through to the upper surface.

Although this is a bit time-consuming, it is well worth the effort, considering the many advantages the canvas offers.

When working on a larger piece without an embroidery frame, roll the canvas under. Hold the rolled canvas in one hand and stitch with the other (see Figure 3).

If it is necessary to join two pieces of canvas, as is required for the Vexar rug in this book, overlap four ridges of canvas and work a row of cross-stitch over the overlapping area. When embroidering that area, stitch through both layers. The joining will not be visible when the project is completed.

EQUIPMENT

Embroidery Frame: Because plastic canvas does not stretch or pull out of shape, the only advantage in working on a frame is speed. It allows you to stitch with both hands by keeping one hand above and one hand below the

Figure 4

surface to push the needle through (see Figure 4). When attaching canvas to a frame, use string or yarn that is not too sharp or hard, and keep an even tension so that it does not cut through the canvas.

Scissors: Two pairs of scissors are recommended, a small one for cutting yarn and a sturdier pair for cutting canvas (see Figure 5). When cutting out a shape, it takes less effort to turn the canvas rather than the scissors.

Needles: For most of the projects I used either a size 18 or size 20 tapestry needle. The size 18 is larger and easier to thread; number 20, because it is finer, slides through the holes a bit more smoothly. Experiment with both and choose the size you find more effective.

Figure 5

·2·

HOME ACCESSORIES

WELCOME PICTURE

MATERIALS

One sheet of 7-mesh Fashion Ease plastic canvas, 11 by 14 inches
Persian yarn (approx.):
  1½ ounces of light blue for background
  ¼ ounce of dark red
  ¼ ounce of black
  Several yards each of olive green, purple, brown, orange, white, bright
    yellow, lemon yellow, bright red, and tan
Tapestry needle, size 18
Lightweight fabric for backing, 12 by 15 inches (optional)

INSTRUCTIONS

1. Cut out edge design on top and both sides of sheet as shown in the graph;
   the bottom side remains as is.

2. Embroider the design in cross-stitch by following the graph.

3. With scissors cut out the windows. Count carefully before cutting. Be
   sure to leave the crossbars. It is important to make a smooth edge.

4. Use an overcast stitch along the edges of each window; wrap yarn around
   each crossbar, covering it completely.

5. To finish the picture, use an overcast stitch with black wool, doubled,
   along all four sides. Remember to stitch into outer corners three times.

6. Make a cord of approximately 16 inches by twisting black wool (see
   page 126). Sew on where shown in the photograph.

Graph 1

□ light blue	V purple	x bright yellow
● dark red	I brown	z lemon yellow
◣ black	o orange	R bright red
/ olive green	W white	+ tan

7. Although it is not essential, I recommend sewing on a backing. It gives the picture a neater appearance. Cut fabric the same size as the canvas. Fold ⅛ inch under and slip stitch to picture. See Plate 1.

ADDITIONAL IDEA

Instead of cutting out the windows, use cross-stitch to outline the windows and crossbars. Fill in the remaining spaces with the same bright red wool as that used in the door.

TREE WALL HANGING

MATERIALS

Two sheets of 7-mesh Fashion Ease plastic canvas, 11 by 14 inches each
Persian yarn (approx.):
    $2\frac{1}{2}$ ounces of apple green
    $1\frac{1}{2}$ ounces of slate gray
Tapestry needle, size 18
Paper to enlarge outline of tree
Ten small bronze Indian bells
Metal or wooden rod for hanging, 11 inches long

INSTRUCTIONS

1. The first sheet of canvas is embroidered entirely in Parisian stitch, using a double strand of apple green yarn. This forms the back panel.

2. The second sheet of canvas is for the tree. Enlarge the outline from the drawing to fit the back panel; cut it out and tape the tree in three or four places to the sheet of canvas. With a waterproof pen lightly mark the outline of the tree. Discard the paper. Cut out the tree, following the outline on the canvas. Try to retain the roundness at the ends of the branches; this gives the design a softer look and makes it easier to embroider. Also, when cutting around corners, it is easier to turn the canvas rather than the scissors.

3. To embroider the tree use an overcast stitch in slate gray, a double strand. Start at the lower right bottom of the trunk. Work up the right side of the tree trunk, around all the branches, and down the other side.

Graph 2

Make the stitches of irregular length; that gives the tree an interesting texture. For example: one stitch over five mesh, next stitch over seven, then over four, and so on. Occasionally stitch into one hole twice, to assure tight coverage. When working on the trunk, reduce your stitches since the trunk becomes narrower. For the branches the overcast stitches will cover only one or two mesh. When these steps have been completed, there will still be two areas (the upper and lower ends of the trunk) that require a few additional stitches. Fill in these areas with straight stitches.

4. Sew the little bells to the branches, distributing them unevenly.

5. Using only one ply of a three-ply strand, attach the tree to the back panel with only occasional stitches. This will add to the three-dimensional quality of the hanging.

6. Cut two strips of canvas, 5 by 1½ inches each (using the leftover trimmings from the tree). Embroider both the same way as the back panel.

7. Use slate gray in a double strand to overcast the edges of the back panel and the strips.

8. Fold strips in half to form a loop. Measure in 1½ inches from each top corner and sew to the back panel. Insert rod and hang. See Plate 2.

ADDITIONAL IDEA

Instead of using bells, attach ceramic or clay beads.

PICTURE FRAMES

FRAME I: BRICK STITCH

MATERIALS

One sheet of 7-mesh Fashion Ease plastic canvas, 11 by 14 inches
Persian yarn (approx.):
    22 yards of olive green
    16 yards each of purple, lavender, medium blue, and light blue
Tapestry needle, size 18
Fabric for lining, in blue or purple, 11 by 14 inches (optional)

INSTRUCTIONS

1. Mark the center of the four sides of the sheet by tying threads at each
   end of the center ridges. (To locate center, simply bend canvas in half.)

2. All areas require double-strand thread and are worked in brick stitch.
   The following directions apply for each side. Begin at the edge, overcasting with olive green yarn next to the previously marked center
   mesh, alternating one stitch over one mesh, one stitch over two mesh.
   Repeat this sequence until the corners are reached.

3. The next inner nine rows are embroidered in brick stitch over two
   mesh. Put the stitches into the spaces of the previous row. Note that
   rows 1 (purple), 2 (lavender), 3 (medium blue), 4 (light blue), and 5
   (olive green) decrease progressively by one stitch on each side of center.
   Rows 6 (light blue), 7 (medium blue), 8 (lavender), and 9 (purple) in-

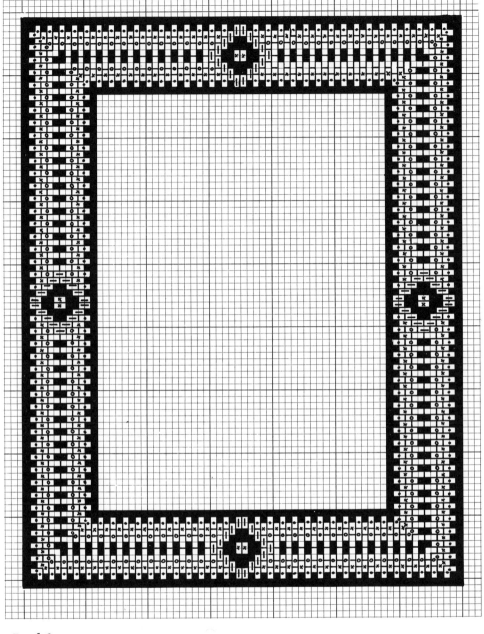

Graph 3

- ■ olive green
- ● purple
- ○ medium blue
- □ light blue
- ✕ lavender

crease progressively by one stitch on each side of center. This decrease and increase of stitches results in an empty diamond, which will be filled in later (see graph).

4. With scissors cut out the inside of the frame. Be sure to leave one row of mesh. This is filled with overcast stitching in olive green (one stitch over one mesh and one over two), as was done with the outer edge of the frame.

5. To fill in the diamond, work a row of brick stitch all around in light blue. The next row is stitched in olive green in the same manner, and the two center stitches are lavender (see graph).

6. To finish, mount picture inside frame with tape. If you wish, the back of the frame can be lined with fabric. Fold the lining ⅛ inch under and slip stitch all around. See Plate 3.

To hang frame you can do one of the following: make a cord by twisting together some embroidery yarn in a matching color and sew onto the two top corners; or wrap a large curtain ring with matching embroidery yarn and sew onto the top center of the frame. The frame can also be used as picture matting; in that case, add a narrow frame of wood or metal.

FRAME II: GOBELIN STITCH

MATERIALS

One sheet of 7-mesh Fashion Ease plastic canvas, 11 by 14 inches
Persian yarn (approx.):
    30 yards of olive green
    20 yards of light green
    18 yards of yellow
Tapestry needle, size 18
Fabric in coordinating color for lining, 11 by 14 inches (optional)

INSTRUCTIONS

1. This frame is embroidered in straight Gobelin stitch with double-strand yarn. There are three rows of stitches to be worked.

2. The first row requires olive green yarn. The stitches are worked in the sequence of two stitches over two mesh and two stitches over four mesh. An inner jagged edge will result all around. At the corner compensate your stitches in order to retain the pattern, as shown in the graph. The second row is light green. All stitches are worked over four threads. This row has a bricklike effect. The third row is worked in yellow in the same manner as the first one, two stitches over two mesh and two stitches over four mesh. A straight edge will now appear.

3. Cut out the inside of the frame, but leave two ridges.

4. With olive green yarn overcast the two inside rows and the outside edge of the frame.

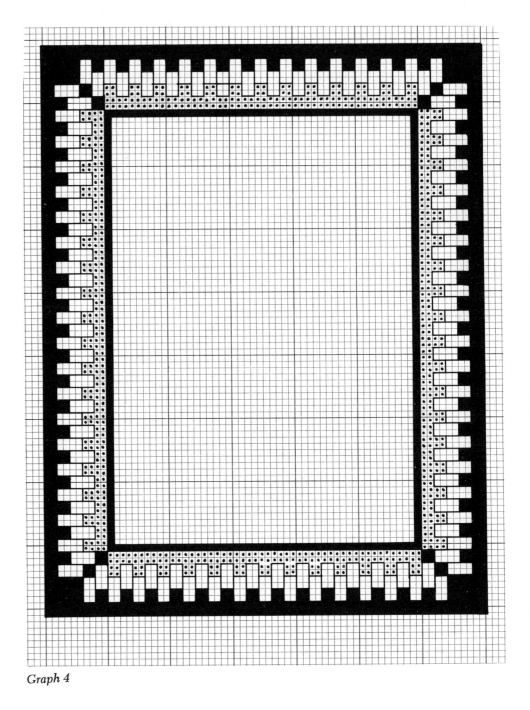

Graph 4

■ olive green   □ light green   • yellow

5. Continue using olive green and cover the empty mesh at the mitered corners with short forward stitches from the outer to the inner edge.

6. For lining and hanging instructions, refer to instructions for Frame I. See Plate 3.

FRAME III: DIAGONAL SCOTCH STITCH

MATERIALS

One sheet of 7-mesh Fashion Ease plastic canvas, 11 by 14 inches
Persian yarn (approx.):
    40 yards of dark gray
    10 yards each of fuchsia, hot pink, rose, and pale pink
Tapestry needle, size 18
Fabric in coordinating color for lining, 11 by 14 inches (optional)

INSTRUCTIONS

1. Mark the center of all four sides of the sheet by tying threads at each
   end of the center ridges. (To locate center, simply bend canvas in half.)
   This ridge remains bare until the Scotch stitch is completed (see step
   5). All areas require double-strand yarn.

2. The frame is embroidered in three rows of diagonal Scotch stitch. Each
   Scotch unit, for this project, is worked over a four-mesh square, which
   will require seven stitches.

3. Begin at corners and work toward the center of each side. In the first
   row the four outer stitches are embroidered in dark gray, the other
   three of the unit in fuchsia. In the second row the unit consists of three
   stitches in hot pink, the center stitch in gray, and the last three in rose.
   The third row uses three stitches of pale pink and four of dark gray for
   each unit (see graph).

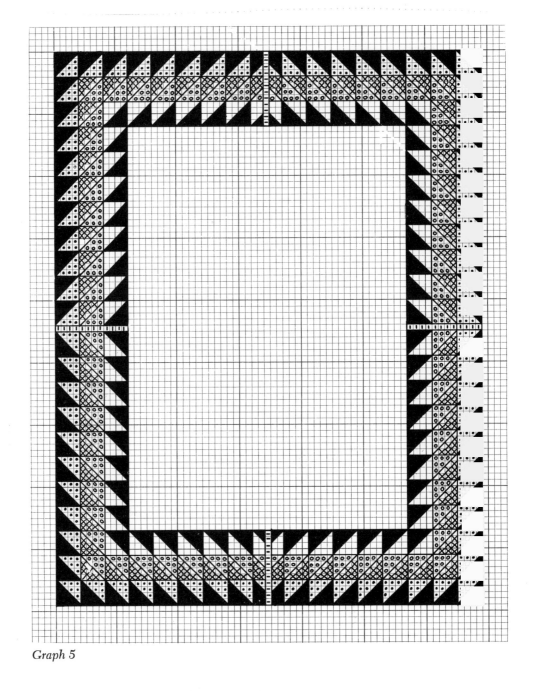

Graph 5

● dark gray   ✗ hot pink   □ pale pink

◢ fuchsia   ○ rose

4. Now carefully cut out the inside of the frame. Be sure to leave one row of mesh for overcasting.

5. With a double strand of gray yarn cover outer and inner edges of frame in overcast stitch. Cover the center ridge of each side with short straight stitches, also in gray.

6. For lining and hanging directions refer to instructions for Frame I. See Plate 3.

MIRROR FRAME

MATERIALS

One piece of 10-mesh Vexar plastic canvas, 13 by 13 inches
Persian yarn (approx.):
      1 ounce of light gray
      1 ounce of light blue
      1 ounce of light turquoise
      30 yards of light turquoise for twisted cord
Tapestry needle, size 20
Mirror tile 3 inches square*
Epoxy glue
All-purpose glue

INSTRUCTIONS

1. Mark the outline of the mirror frame with a waterproof pen. Also outline the square where the mirror tile will be glued (see graph).

2. The frame is embroidered in mosaic stitch. Begin at an inner corner (marked for mirror tile) and with light gray yarn stitch a row of mosaic toward outer corner of the frame. Also embroider a row diagonally across outer corner (see step 1 on the graph). Repeat this for the other three corners. These are the main rows and they establish the design.

3. Continue by embroidering a row of blue, then a row of turquoise on each side of these main rows (see step 2 on the graph). Repeat this color

*This can be cut to size by your local glazier.

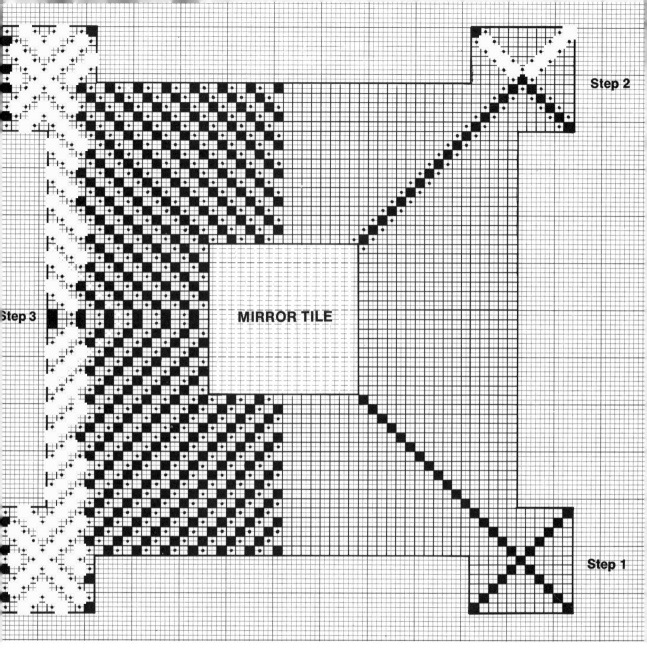

Step 2

Step 3

MIRROR TILE

Step 1

Graph 6

■ light gray   ● light blue   □ light turquoise

1 square = 1 mosaic stitch

sequence of gray, blue, and turquoise until all rows meet in the center of the four sides of the frame (see step 3 on the graph).

4. Leave one ridge for overcasting when cutting away the outer unembroidered area.

5. With turquoise yarn make an overcast stitch along the edges of the frame.

6. Use epoxy glue to fasten the mirror tile over the unembroidered center square. To assure permanence, weight the tile down with a book or a similar object and leave in place overnight.

7. Twist a cord of turquoise yarn (see page 126). Fasten the cord with all-purpose glue around the mirror tile and to the outside edges of the frame. Use double-sided self-sticking tape to attach to the wall. See Plate 4.

TISSUE BOX COVER

MATERIALS

Five pieces of 10-mesh Vexar plastic canvas: one piece, 10½ by 5¼ inches,
 for the top; two pieces, 10½ by 5 inches, for the front and back; and two
 pieces, 5¼ by 5 inches, for the sides
Persian yarn (approx.):
    1½ ounces of light gray
    1½ ounces of light blue
    1½ ounces of light turquoise
Tapestry needle, size 20

INSTRUCTIONS

1. Before beginning, be sure to compare the dimensions of the tissue box
    with those of the brand of facial tissue you generally buy. This cover
    fits most brands. For smaller or larger boxes, decrease or increase
    accordingly.

2. *Top:* Mark the inside area of the top panel with a waterproof pen. This
    will later be cut out. Also mark the center of the panel, located by
    folding it in half.

3. Starting from the center, establish in gray yarn the first diagonal rows
    on each half of the top, as the graph indicates. Continue filling in the
    rows in the proper color sequence of gray, blue, and turquoise.

4. *Front, back, and sides:* As with the top panel of the tissue box cover,
    first locate the center of each panel and embroider a row of gray mosaic
    on each half side (see graph). Fill in the rest of the design as indicated.

5. Leave one ridge around each panel and if necessary trim away excess canvas.

6. With one ridge again remaining, cut out the marked inside area of the top as an opening for the tissues. Finish the edge of the opening with a turquoise overcast stitch.

7. In turquoise overcasting join the front and back panels to the sides. Add the top of the cover in the same manner. Overcast all along the bottom edges.

8. Some tissue boxes have oval openings. In that case, trim away some of the cardboard so that it does not show through the opening. See Plate 4.

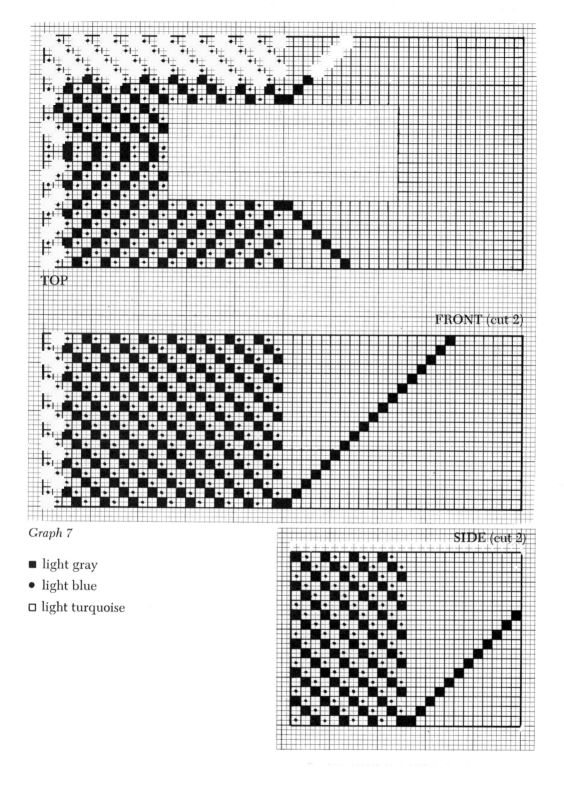

TOP

FRONT (cut 2)

Graph 7

■ light gray
● light blue
□ light turquoise

SIDE (cut 2)

BUTTERFLY PLACE MAT

MATERIALS

One piece of 10-mesh Vexar plastic canvas, 15 by 19 inches
Persian yarn (approx.):

1 ounce of purple	*or*	1 ounce of rose
1 ounce of lavender		1 ounce of pink
1 ounce of dark turquoise		1 ounce of dark peacock blue
1 ounce of light turquoise		1 ounce of light peacock blue
½ ounce of dark green		½ ounce of black
1 thread of yellow		(as shown on book jacket)

Tapestry needle, size 20
Dark green fabric for lining, 15 by 19 inches (optional)

INSTRUCTIONS

1. Fold the canvas in half to locate the center. Using the center line as a reference, lightly outline the body and wings of the butterfly with a waterproof pen.

2. *Body:* Embroider dark green areas in continental stitch, purple and dark turquoise areas in Parisian (see graph). Add two continental stitches in yellow for eyes.

Graph 8—opposite

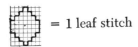 = 1 leaf stitch

    □ purple   ○ light turquoise

    × lavender   ■ dark green

    v dark turquoise   Y yellow

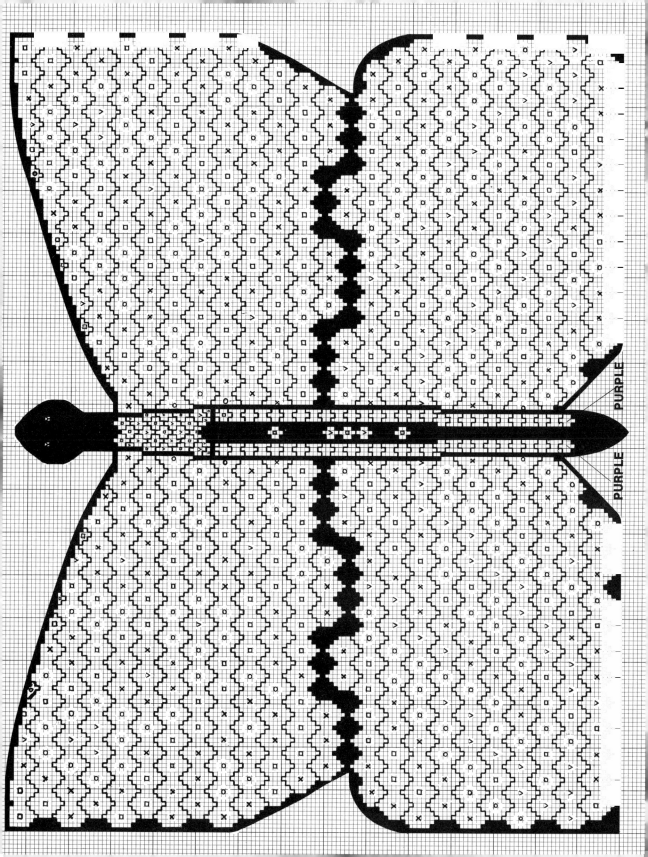

PURPLE

PURPLE

3. *Wings:* Embroider, using the colors indicated in the graph, in leaf stitch with the exception of the dark green horizontal area at the center of the wings and also along the edges. Note two necessary procedures: First, in order to achieve a fairly smooth outline, compensate leaf stitches as indicated on the graph, particularly along the top edge and at certain points along the sides. Second, point the stitches for the top areas of the wings up, and for the bottom areas down.

4. The dark green horizontal area is completed in continental stitch. The same stitch is used to fill in the sides and bottom edges.

5. Cut out the butterfly, but leave one ridge. Use overcast stitch with dark green yarn all along the edge of the butterfly.

6. *Lining:* Cut out the fabric in the same dimensions as the butterfly. Tuck ⅛ inch under and slip stitch to the canvas. See Plate 5.

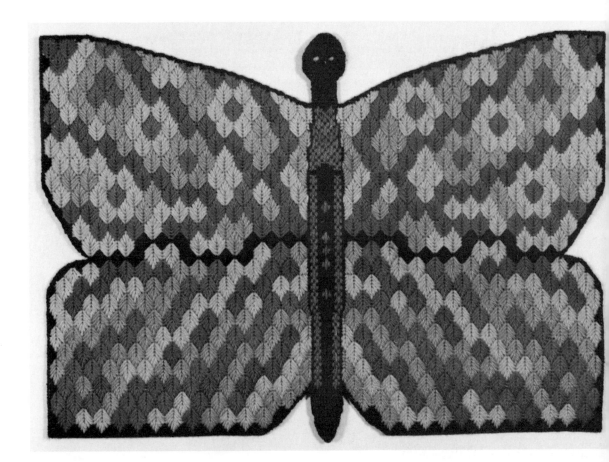

BUTTERFLY NAPKIN RING

MATERIALS

One piece of 10-mesh Vexar plastic canvas, 2 by 6 inches
Persian yarn (approx.):
>   10 yards lavender
>   Several threads of purple, light turquoise, dark turquoise, and dark
>   green

Tapestry needle, size 20
Cross-grained ribbon in lavender, 2 by 6½ inches (optional)

INSTRUCTIONS

1. Center the design on the canvas and outline the butterfly in purple,
   using continental stitch. Embroider on each wing three leaf stitches in
   dark turquoise (see graph). Fill in the rest of the wings in purple continental stitch. Use dark green for the body.

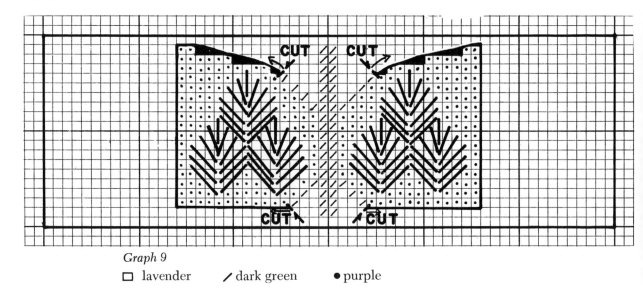

Graph 9
□ lavender   / dark green   • purple

2. To separate the wings from the background, leave one ridge all around and carefully cut from one arrow to the other (see graph).

3. Embroider the background in lavender continental stitch.

4. Use dark green yarn and overcast stitch along the edges of the wings. Apply overcasting in light turquoise to finish the long edges of the napkin ring.

5. *Lining*: Pin ribbon to the wrong side of the embroidered area, fold the raw edges under, and slip stitch.

6. Bring the two narrow edges together to form a ring and bind stitch together with lavender yarn. See Plate 5.

FLOWER COASTERS

MATERIALS

One piece of 10-mesh Vexar plastic canvas, 5 by 5 inches, for each coaster
Persian yarn (approx.):

    ½ ounce of color of your choice (when making a set, use a variety of colors)

    A few strands of black and white

Tapestry needle, size 20
Colored felt for backing (optional)

INSTRUCTIONS

1. Using continental stitch, establish the outline of the coaster with your main color. Follow the graph as a guide.

2. Embroider the center of the coaster in black and white. Then fill in the remaining area in the same color as the outline.

3. Leave one ridge and trim away excess canvas. Finish the coaster with an overcast stitch in black yarn.

4. A backing of color-coordinated felt can be slip stitched to the finished coaster. See Plate 6.

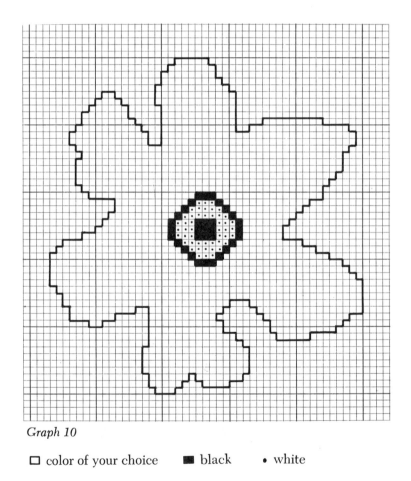

Graph 10

□ color of your choice   ■ black   • white

VEXAR (Free-Form) RUG

MATERIALS

One piece of 5-mesh Vexar plastic canvas, 50 by 60 inches (in case you have difficulty obtaining the necessary width for this project, see page 14 for instructions on how to join two pieces of canvas together)

Paterna rug yarn (approx.):

28 ounces of brown
16 ounces of olive green
14 ounces of lemon yellow
14 ounces of light blue
10 ounces of white
 8 ounces of medium blue
 8 ounces of medium yellow
 6 ounces of orange
 5 ounces of light yellow

Rug needle
Fabric for lining (optional)

INSTRUCTIONS

1. The rug is completely worked in diagonal Scotch stitch. Mark the center of the width, and three rows below begin the pattern with brown wool to establish the design (see graph).

2. Follow the graph, which represents one-fourth of the complete rug. Continue working toward the long edges by stitching one row in pale yellow, two rows in medium yellow, one row in orange, two rows in white, one row in medium blue, two rows in light blue, two rows in lemon yellow, three rows in green, and the last row again in brown.

3. Next, fill in the three empty areas along the center with brown and green wool.

4. The four pointed areas in each quarter are also worked in brown and green.

5. Leave one ridge for binding stitch and cut away excess canvas. Using brown wool, work binding stitch all around.

6. Make thirty-six tassels (see page 126) in brown for two sides of the rug. Each tassel is 8 inches long and contains twenty threads. Space evenly and sew on where indicated on the graph. Next make an additional four tassels from leftover colored yarn, adding a few strands of brown. They are also 8 inches long but contain forty threads each. Sew on each side of the four pointed areas, as shown on the graph. See Plate 7.

7. If you wish, the rug can be lined with a nonskid fabric.

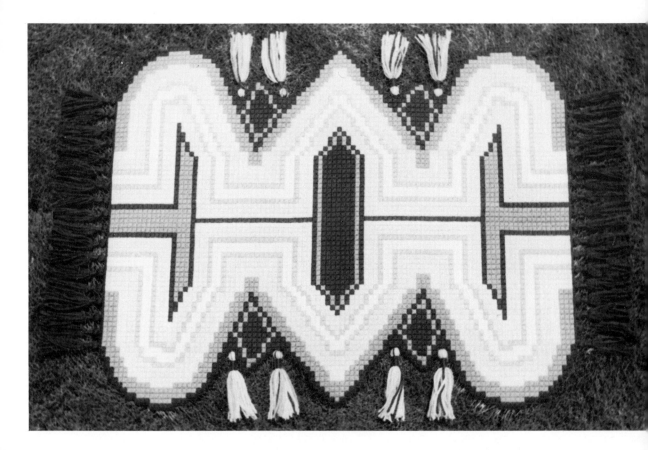

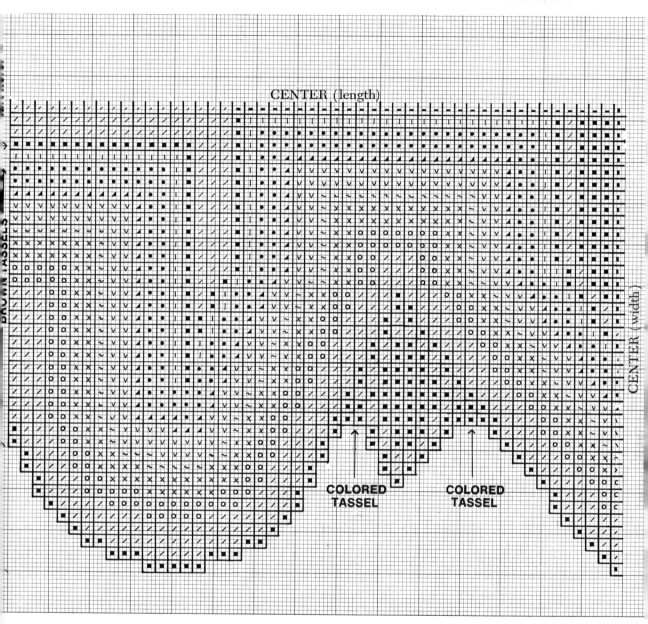

Graph 11

■ brown	✕ light blue	◢ orange
╱ olive green	~ medium blue	● medium yellow
○ lemon yellow	v white	ı light yellow

GEOMETRIC RUG

MATERIALS

Six sheets of 7-mesh Fashion Ease plastic canvas, 11 by 14 inches each
Persian yarn for each panel (approx.):
  3 ounces of light gray
  1 ounce of bright red
  1 ounce of dark red
Tapestry needle, size 20
Fabric for lining in the same size as the rug (optional)

INSTRUCTIONS

1. This rug is made up of six panels. It can be enlarged by adding panels. Multiply the amount of yarn required for one panel by the number of panels you plan to use.

    Doubled yarn is necessary for both the continental stitch (the background) and the rice stitch (the design).

2. First fill in the five vertical and one horizontal rows in gray continental stitch, as indicated by the arrows in the graph. These rows are part of the background.

3. For the design, a rice stitch (consisting of a cross-stitch and tie-downs) is used. First, the cross-stitch is done in dark red. Second, the tie-downs are worked in bright red. Reverse the reds of the stitches so that the colors of each panel alternate.

4. Fill in the rest of the background with gray continental stitches.

5. When the number of desired panels have been completed, join them to-

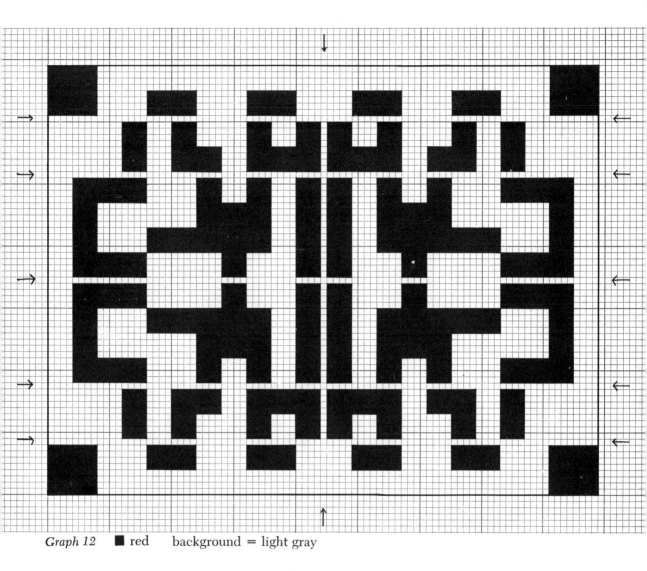

Graph 12   ■ red   background = light gray

gether with binding stitch, using dark red single-strand yarn. Finish the edges also with binding stitch.

6. If you wish to attach a fringe, use the dark red yarn. Cut yarn to 7-inch lengths. Fold two strands in half to form a loop. With a crochet hook pull loop from front of rug through the back. Push ends into the loop and pull tight. Trim ends to even length.

7. *Lining:* Cut fabric to the same size as rug. Fold ⅛ inch under and slip stitch to the rug. See Plate 8.

ADDITIONAL IDEA

A single embroidered panel also makes an attractive wall hanging (see photograph). Bind stitch all around in red. Add red tassels at the bottom. To hang, wrap two curtain rings with red yarn and sew to the two top corners.

·3·

DESK
ACCESSORIES

TYPEWRITER COVER

MATERIALS

Three pieces of 10-mesh Vexar plastic canvas: one piece 13 by 24 inches,
   and two pieces 7 by 14 inches
Persian yarn (approx.):
      8 ounces of black
      6 ounces of white
Tapestry needle, size 20
Lightweight black fabric, ¾ yard, 36 inches wide, for lining (optional)

INSTRUCTIONS

1. The cover is designed for a standard electric portable typewriter. Before you begin, compare the measurements with the typewriter you
   wish to cover; adjust proportions if necessary.

2. On graph paper enlarge the pattern for the two side panels to actual
   size. With waterproof pen trace on plastic canvas and cut out two side
   panels. Measure and cut out center panel.

3. Use continental stitch for the entire piece. Fill in the black design first,
   then the white areas.

   Center panel: Locate the center of panel by folding the canvas in half
lengthwise and mark with a thread or waterproof pen. Begin the design at
the center of the front edge (see graph) and stitch toward each side, following the pattern. The design looks more complicated than it is. Once a
complete repeat is established, the stitching requires a minimum of con-
centration. Repeat the pattern until all 24 inches are filled.

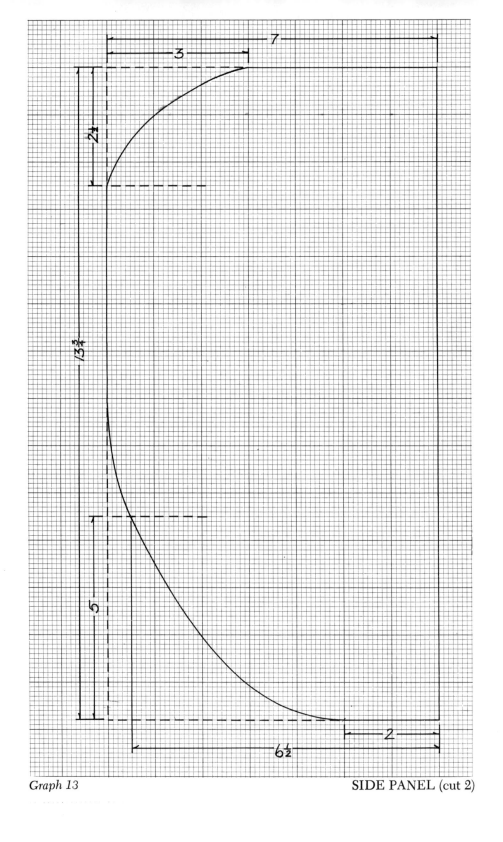

Graph 13   SIDE PANEL (cut 2)

Side panel: Be sure to mark the side panels as right and left so that you don't end up with two for one side and none for the other. This pattern is extremely simple (see graph). Again, it is easier to stitch the black areas before filling in the rest with white.

4. *Cover lining:* Cut the material for the center and each side panel the same size as the pattern. Lay the linings over the panels, fold ⅛ inch under, and slip stitch all around.

5. To assemble, use an overcast stitch to join side panels to the center piece. Also use overcast stitching for baseline.

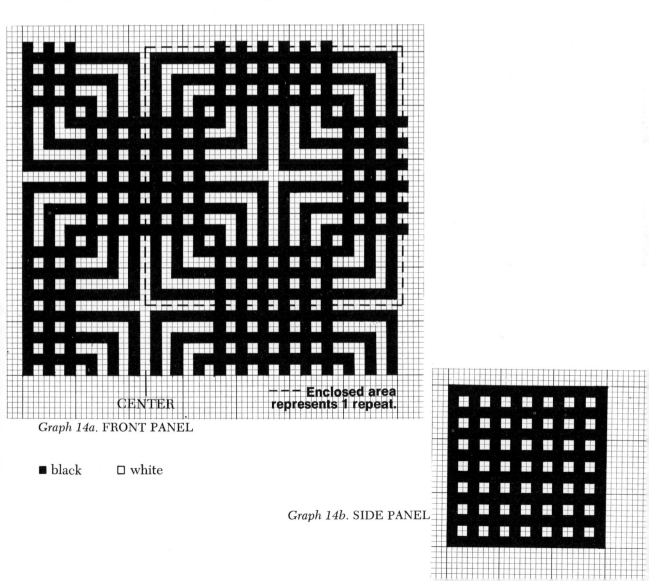

--- **Enclosed area represents 1 repeat.**

CENTER

Graph 14a. FRONT PANEL

■ black   □ white

Graph 14b. SIDE PANEL

DESK PAD

MATERIALS

Three pieces of 10-mesh Vexar plastic canvas: two pieces 5½ by 19 inches,
   and one piece 19 by 30 inches
Persian yarn:
   2½ ounces of black
      2 ounces of white
Tapestry needle, size 20
White or black blotting paper, 19 by 30 inches

INSTRUCTIONS

1. The large piece of canvas is used as the back panel and is not embroidered.

2. *Left and right panels:* Embroider the two panels in continental stitch by following the graph of the typewriter cover (top). Stitch the black design first, then fill in the white. Note that one of the panels must have the pattern reversed to complement the other (see photograph).

3. Make an overcast stitch in black along the inner side of each panel.

4. Place the embroidered panels over each short side of the large piece of canvas so that each row of overcasting faces inward.

5. Use an overcast stitch to join left and right panels to the back. Continue overcasting along the top and bottom edges of the back panel.

6. Insert the paper blotter (trim if necessary) into the two side panels.

STAMP BOX

MATERIALS

Two pieces of 10-mesh Vexar plastic canvas, 8 by 8 inches and 5½ by 5½
  inches
Persian yarn (approx.):
    1½ ounces of black
    ½ ounce of white
Tapestry needle, size 20
¼ yard of lightweight black fabric (optional)

INSTRUCTIONS

1. *Base:* Embroider the design in continental stitch as shown in the graph.
   (Note that there is only one row of black along sides and top.)

2. Leave one ridge all around and trim away excess areas. Put aside.

3. *Cover:* Embroider the box top according to the graph. Trim, but leave
   one ridge.

4. *Lining:* Cut the fabric the same size as the two embroidered panels.
   Before slip stitching fabric to panels, clip the lining a tiny bit at the
   inner corners so that the raw edges fold under more smoothly.

5. To assemble, fold the corners of the box and cover so that the points of
   each corner come together (indicated by numbers on the graph) and
   bind stitch in black. Also use binding stitch along the edges of the base
   and of the cover. See photo, page 58.

Plate 1. Welcome Picture

Plate 2. Tree Wall Hanging

Plate 3. Picture Frames

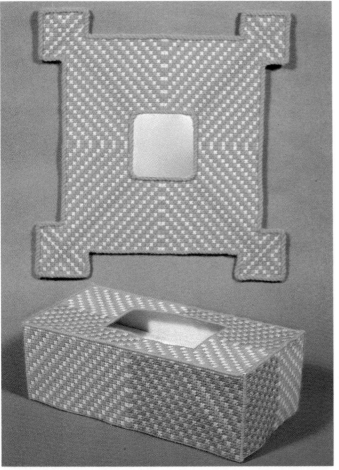

Plate 4. Mirror Frame and Tissue Box Cover

Plate 5. Butterfly Place Mat and Napkin Ring

Plate 6. Flower Coasters

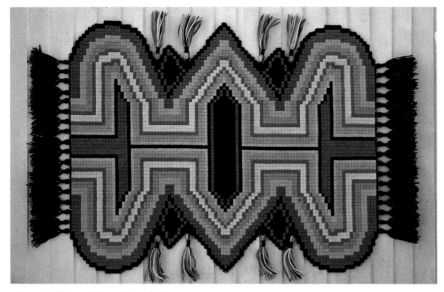

Plate 7. Vexar (Free-Form) Rug

Plate 8. Geometric Rug

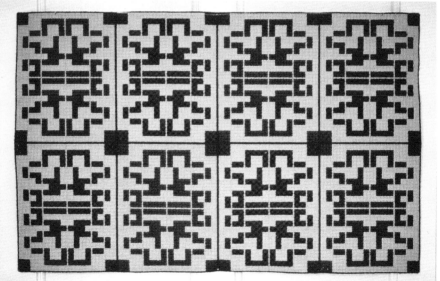

Plate 9. Belt

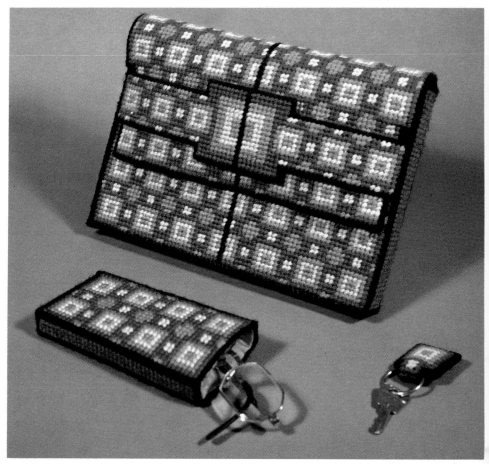

Plate 10. Clutch Bag, Eyeglasses Case, Key Holder

Plate 11. Carrying Bag

Plate 12. Sewing Box, Scissors Case, Pincushion, Trinket Box

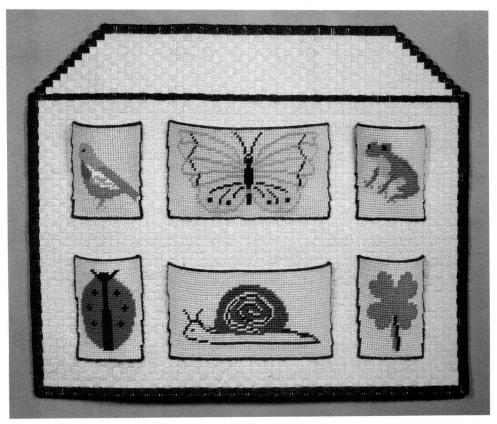

Plate 13. Wall Organizer

Plate 14. Potted Flowers

Plate 15. Lizzy Doll

Plate 16. Photo Album Cover

Plate 17. Straw Basket

Plate 18. Alphabet Letters

Plate 19. Embroidered Alphabet Sculpture

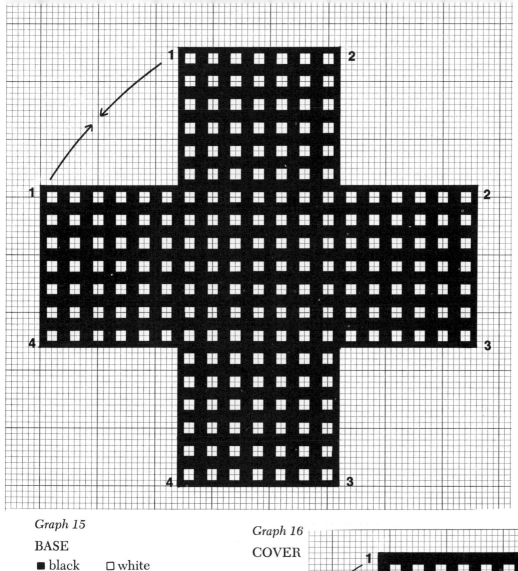

Graph 15

BASE

■ black   □ white

Graph 16

COVER

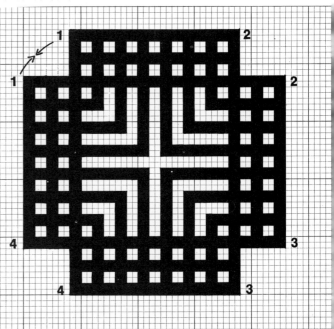

ADDITIONAL IDEA

You can make the box without the cover. Insert a waterproof container and use as a small vase or flower pot holder (see photo, page 58).

CHECKBOOK COVER

MATERIALS

One piece of 10-mesh Vexar plastic canvas, 7 by 7 inches
Persian yarn (approx.):
 20 yards of black
 12 yards of white
Tapestry needle, size 20
22 inches of black satin ribbon, 2½ inches wide

INSTRUCTIONS

1. Compare the measurements of the cover with your checkbook. If necessary, increase or decrease the dimensions.

2. Begin at the front center and embroider the design in continental stitch
   according to the graph. Stitch first the black areas, then the rest of the
   pattern in white.

3. Leaving one ridge along edge, trim off excess canvas.

4. Cut the satin ribbon into three pieces of equal length. Place the embroidered panel wrong side up. Fold a piece of ribbon lengthwise and
   place it so that this fold matches the fold line of the cover (see graph).
   Tuck the raw edges under and stitch down along all four sides.

5. Keeping the panel wrong side up, put the second piece of ribbon along
   the upper edge of the cover. Tuck the raw edges under. Stitch three
   sides of the ribbon to the edge of the cover, to create a pocket.

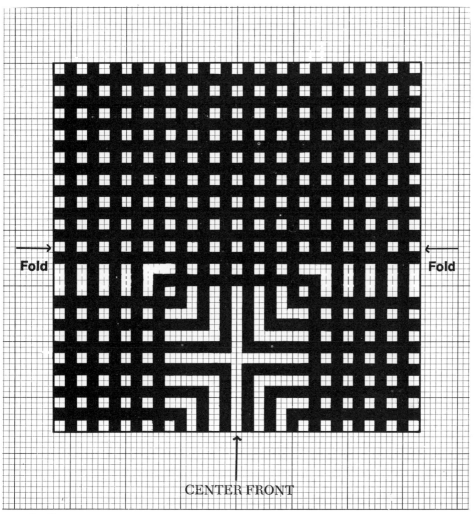

Fold

Fold

CENTER FRONT

Graph 17

 black   □ white

6. Attach the third piece of ribbon in the same way on the lower portion of the cover. You now have a lined inner surface with a pocket in the upper part and one in the lower part of the inside cover in which a checkbook can be placed.

7. Fold the checkbook cover and weight it down overnight so that it stays closed, or sew on a tiny button and loop to fold securely. See photo, page 58.

·4·

PERSONAL ACCESSORIES

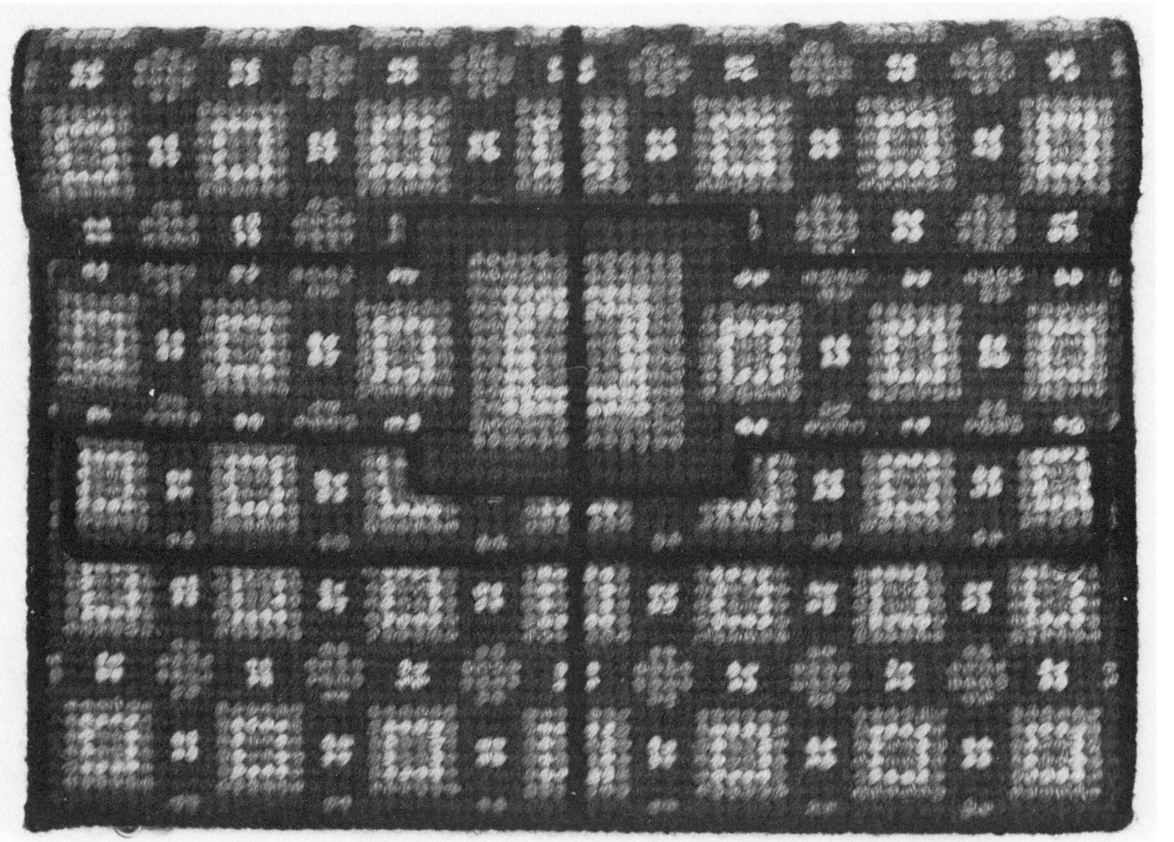

CLUTCH BAG

MATERIALS

Two sheets of 7-mesh Fashion Ease plastic canvas, 11 by 14 inches each
Persian yarn (approx.):
 5 ounces of purple
 3 ounces of rose
 2 ounces of lavender
 ½ ounce of black
Tapestry needle, size 18
Lightweight fabric in rose or lavender, 24 by 15 inches

INSTRUCTIONS

1. All six parts of the bag are worked in continental stitch with double-strand yarn. The first sheet of canvas is used for the back and overlap. To form the overlap, cut away two ridges to the length of 3 inches from both sides of one end of the rectangle (see graph). This is in order for the overlap to be tucked into the latch with greater ease.

2. Stitch one row of black vertically and one row horizontally as indicated on the graph. Next, fill in the design by embroidering in purple first, to establish the pattern, then in rose and lavender.

3. The second sheet of canvas is divided into five parts. Consult the graph and count carefully before cutting the pieces: front part, bottom, two sides, and latch.

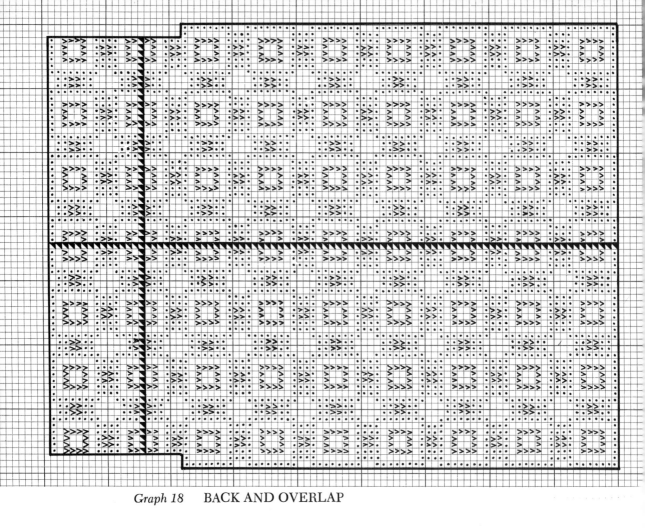

Graph 18 BACK AND OVERLAP

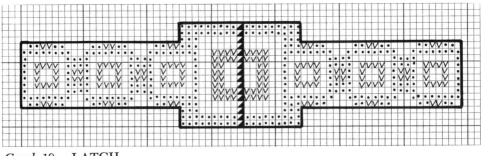

Graph 19 LATCH

● purple   ∨ lavender
□ rose   ◢ black

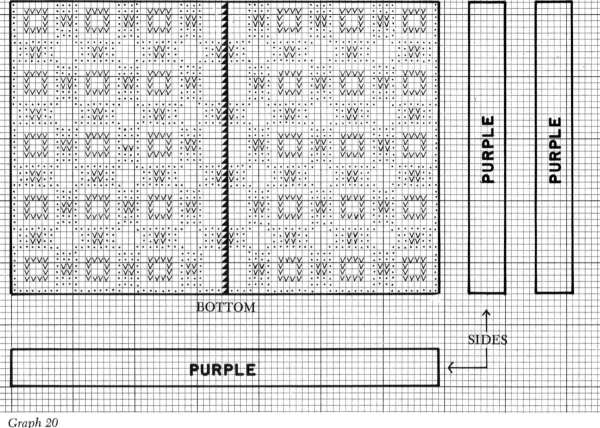

Graph 20

4. Embroider the front part and latch according to the pattern on the graph. The sides and bottom are stitched in purple.

5. It is easier to line the bag before assembling it. Cut the fabric into the same size as each embroidered piece. Fold under ⅛ inch all around and slip stitch.

6. With a binding stitch and single-strand black yarn join the sides and bottom together. Then attach to them the front and back panels. Continue in binding stitch around the bare edges of the bag.

7. Measure 1¾ inches down from top of the front panel and bind stitch the latch to each side of the front panel using a single strand of black. See Plate 10.

EYEGLASSES CASE

MATERIALS

One-half sheet of 7-mesh Fashion Ease plastic canvas, 11 by $6\frac{1}{2}$ inches
Persian yarn (approx.):

$\frac{1}{2}$ ounce of purple
$\frac{1}{4}$ ounce of rose
$\frac{1}{4}$ ounce of lavender
$\frac{1}{4}$ ounce of black

Tapestry needle, size 18
Fabric for lining, 6 by 9 inches

INSTRUCTIONS

1. Double the wool and stitch the front and back panel of the design as shown (see graph) in continental stitch. Work the purple stitches first, then fill in the rose and lavender.

2. Embroider in purple the insets: a bottom and two sides.

3. Cut out all five parts; be sure to leave one ridge all around.

4. Line each piece by cutting the fabric the same size as the embroidered pieces. Tuck $\frac{1}{8}$ inch under all around and slip stitch.

5. Use a binding stitch and black single-strand wool to join insets together. Next, join the two panels to the insets. Finish with a binding stitch along the top of the case. See Plate 10.

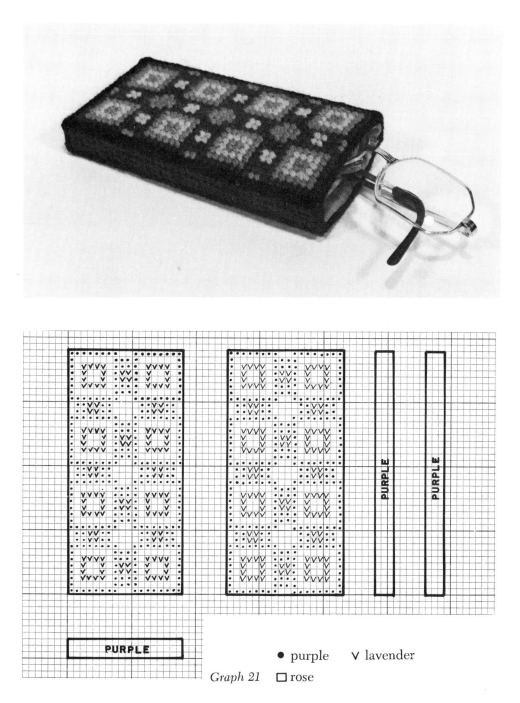

PURPLE

● purple   ∨ lavender

Graph 21   □ rose

KEY HOLDER

MATERIALS

One piece of 7-mesh Fashion Ease plastic canvas, 1½ by 3 inches
Persian yarn: a few strands of purple, rose, lavender, and black
Tapestry needle, size 18
Key ring*

INSTRUCTIONS

1. Double the wool and embroider in continental stitch two repeats of the design as the graph indicates. To establish the outline, work the purple stitches first.

2. Leave one ridge all around and cut out the embroidered area.

3. Insert key ring in the narrow part (center) of the embroidered piece. Fold it together so that the two designs are on top of each other. Then with a black single strand, using binding stitch, join the two layers.

4. Attach your key, or keys, to the ring. See Plate 10.

ADDITIONAL IDEA

Make a whole set of key holders, using your own color code.

*Available at hardware stores.

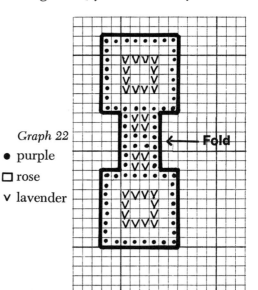

Graph 22

● purple
□ rose
v lavender

BELT

MATERIALS

One piece of 10-mesh Vexar plastic canvas, 3½ by 30 inches (length may
  vary, depending on waistline)
One roll of Dorriespun, three-ply stardust lamé, or other silver thread
D.M.C. cotton perle No. 3 (approx.):

  1 skein of light gray
  1 skein of dark red
  2 skeins of green
  2 skeins of ocher
  3 skeins of dark gray

Tapestry needle, size 20
Silver belt buckle

INSTRUCTIONS

1. Mark the center of the canvas and begin stitching in the lower part of
   the center (back). This is important because the design moves up from
   the base by one ridge after each repeat. It gives the belt a slight upper
   curve toward the front and, consequently, a better fit than when worked
   in straight rows. Use double thread for all areas and embroider in continental stitch, following the graph.

2. Measure waistline and adjust length of belt by adding or subtracting
   part of, or a whole, repeat. This must be done equally on both sides.

3. Cut out the embroidered portion, leaving one ridge for overcasting all

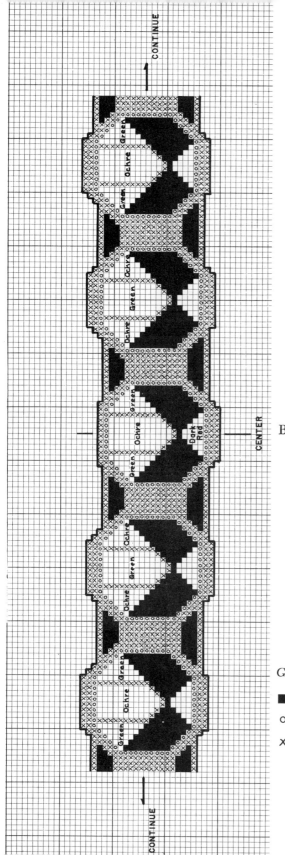

CONTINUE

Green Ochre

Ochre Green

Green Ochre

Ochre Green

Green Ochre

Green Ochre

Dark Red

CENTER BACK

Green Ochre

Ochre Green

Green Ochre

Ochre Green

CONTINUE

around. Use dark gray cotton perle, a double strand, to complete this step.

4. Sew on belt buckle. See Plate 9.

ADDITIONAL IDEAS

Change the indicated colors to coordinate the belt with a favorite dress, or use gold thread instead of silver and add a gold buckle.

Graph 23

■ dark gray

○ light gray

✕ silver

CARRYING BAG

MATERIALS

Three sheets of 7-mesh Fashion Ease plastic canvas, 11 by 14 inches
Two additional strips of the same canvas, $1\frac{1}{2}$ by 14 inches, for handles
Persian yarn (approx.): 5 ounces of bright green
Satin cord: 100 yards of purple
Rhodalure silver cord: 1 skein (10 yards)
Tapestry needle, size 18
$\frac{1}{2}$ yard of fabric, small plaid or print, in green and purple, 36 inches wide
   (optional)

INSTRUCTIONS

1. Two of the sheets are for the panels of the bag. Cut the third sheet
   lengthwise into three 3-inch strips for inset. One is for the bottom, the
   other two for the sides of the bag. Trim the side strips to 14 inches to
   match the height of the bag.

2. To embroider panels and strips use double-strand thread for all green
   areas—background, sides, and bottom of bag—in continental stitch. The
   purple lines are worked in slanted Gobelin. The central design of each
   panel (see graph) is stitched also in continental using the purple satin
   cord and double-strand silver thread.

3. To sew the bag together, use a binding stitch and only a single strand
   of thread. First complete the inset by joining the two sides to the bottom, then add the two panels. Stitch into corners three times to assure
   complete coverage. Add binding stitch along the top of the bag.

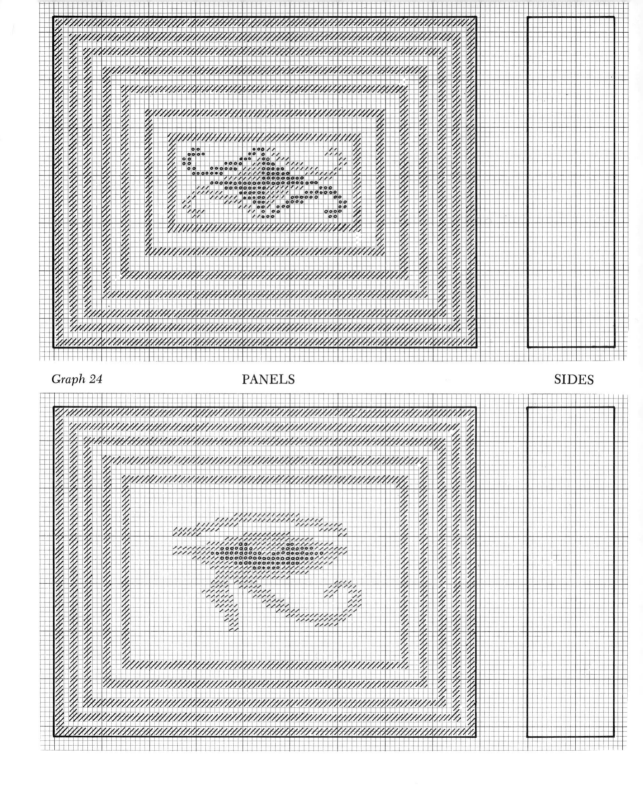

Graph 24 PANELS SIDES

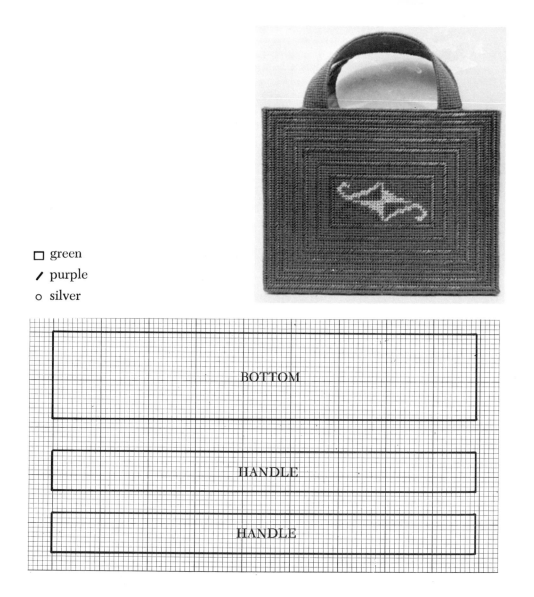

□ green
/ purple
o silver

BOTTOM

HANDLE

HANDLE

4. Embroider handles in continental stitch with double-strand thread. Cover the edges with a binding stitch and sew onto bag. See Plate 11.

ADDITIONAL IDEA

Instead of preparing handles, buy a pair. There are attractive ones made of plastic, bamboo, or metal available in crafts stores. They add an additional touch of elegance to your bag.

WALL ORGANIZER

MATERIALS

Two pieces of 10-mesh Vexar plastic canvas: one piece, 17 by 20 inches, for
the back panel; and one piece, 18 by 12 inches, for the pockets
Persian yarn (approx.):
  6½ ounces of light green
  ½ ounce of dark brown
  Several yards each of red, green, rust, orange, peach, bright red, royal
  blue, light blue, white, dark yellow, light yellow, medium brown,
  and beige
Tapestry needle, size 20
Heavy-duty thread, dark brown

INSTRUCTIONS

1. Embroider the back panel completely in wicker stitch. Establish the
   outline by stitching one row in dark brown wicker all around, plus one
   horizontal row above the pockets (see graph). Fill in the rest of the area
   in light green.

2. Trim the canvas, leaving one ridge; overcast in dark brown.

3. Cut the other piece of canvas into six pockets, referring to the graph for
   measurements, and embroider on each one the indicated motif. All
   pockets are worked in continental stitch.

4. Use overcast stitch in dark brown around all four sides of each pocket.

5. With heavy-duty brown thread sew pockets onto the back panel. In
   each case, attach bottom of pocket first, then pull in the sides so they

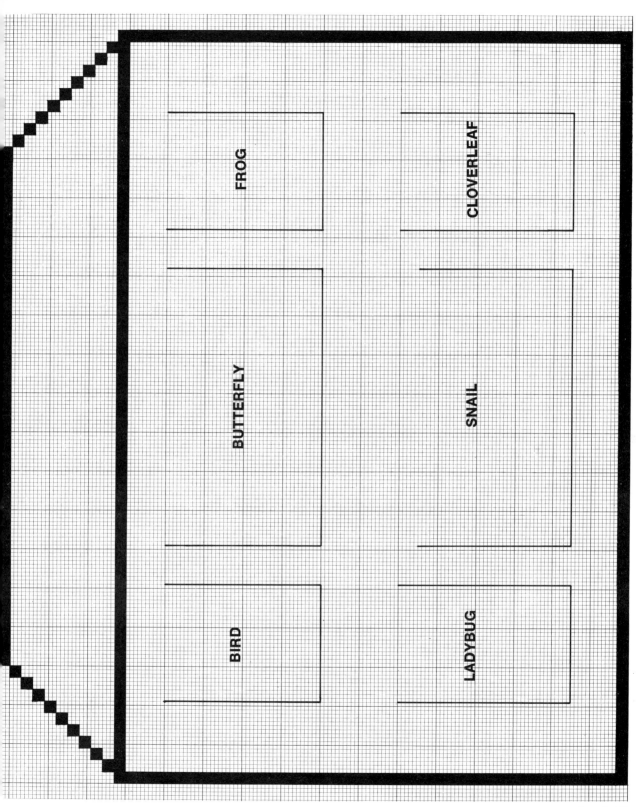

FROG

CLOVERLEAF

BUTTERFLY

SNAIL

BIRD

LADYBUG

Graph 25

form straight vertical lines as indicated on the side view. This will make the pockets protrude on the top and permit larger items to be tucked into them.

6. For hanging, sew two loops on the wrong side of the back panel about 1 inch below the upper corners, or attach two small brown curtain rings directly on the two upper corners. See Plate 13.

7. If you wish to line the wall organizer, cut the fabric in the same size as the back panel, fold ⅛ inch under, and slip stitch to the embroidered panel.

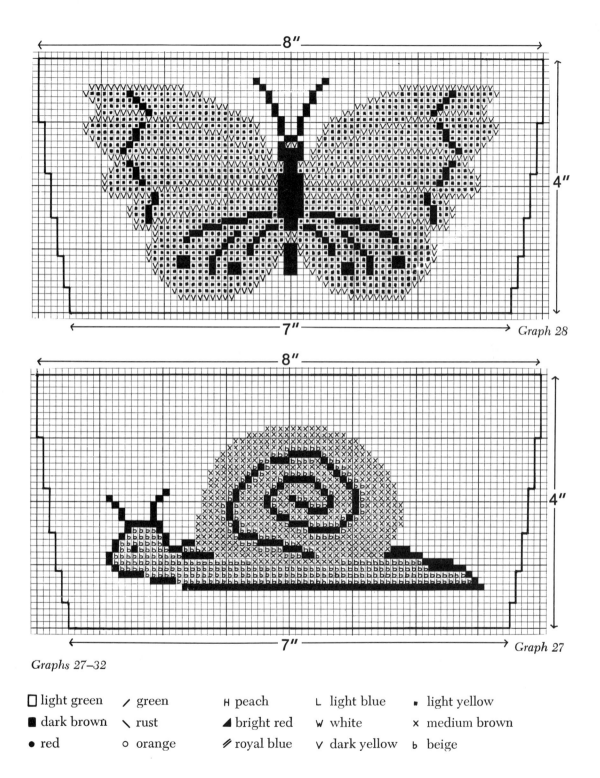

8"

4"

7" ———→ Graph 28

8"

4"

7" ———→ Graph 27

Graphs 27–32

□ light green	⁄ green	ʜ peach	ʟ light blue	▪ light yellow
■ dark brown	＼ rust	◢ bright red	ᴡ white	× medium brown
● red	○ orange	⫽ royal blue	ᴠ dark yellow	♭ beige

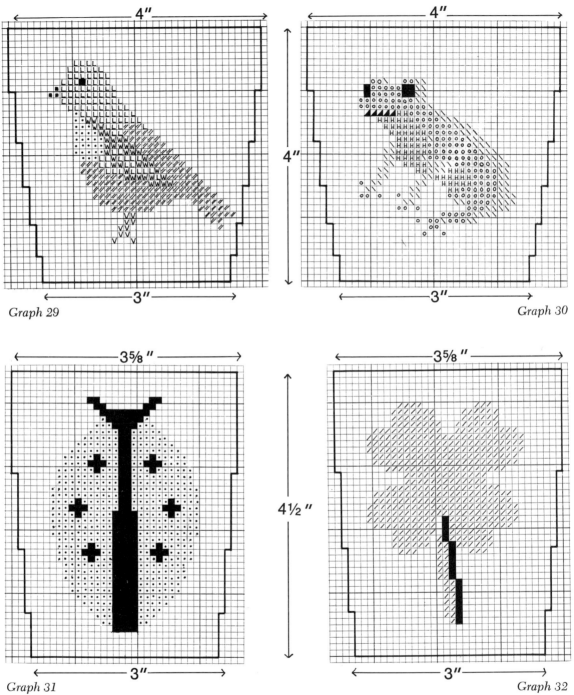

Graph 29

Graph 30

Graph 31

Graph 32

SEWING OR STORAGE BOX

MATERIALS

Four sheets of 7-mesh Fashion Ease plastic canvas, 11 by 14 inches each
Persian yarn (approx.):

> 3 ounces of orange
> 2½ ounces of peach
> 2 ounces of gray

Tapestry needle, size 18
½ yard fabric in a coordinating color, 36 inches wide (optional)

INSTRUCTIONS

1. *Sides:* Cut two sheets into exact halves; this will eliminate the center ridge. Trim off the width to 8 inches. (Do not discard the excess can-

vas; it can be used for smaller projects, such as scissors case, pincushion, or trinket box.)

2. Embroider the four sides. Begin with a single strand of gray and establish the design in cross-stitch. Then fill in the areas between the gray outlines with double-strand thread, using Byzantine stitch and alternate orange and peach colors (see graph).

3. *Bottom:* Cut the third sheet into an 8-inch square. See pattern for the box cover.

4. *Cover:* Embroider the last sheet by following the design on the graph. Leave one ridge all around and cut out the embroidered area.

5. *Lining:* Cut the fabric to the size of each embroidered panel, tuck ⅛ inch under, and slip stitch.

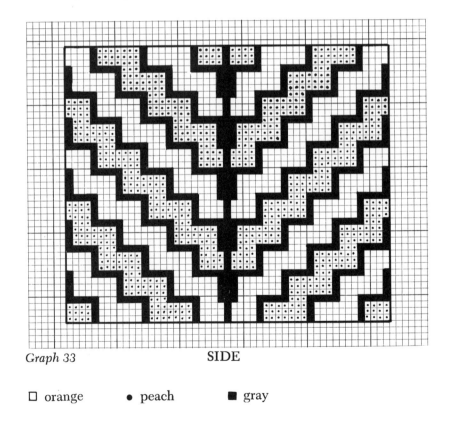

Graph 33　　　　　　　　　**SIDE**

□ orange　　　• peach　　　■ gray

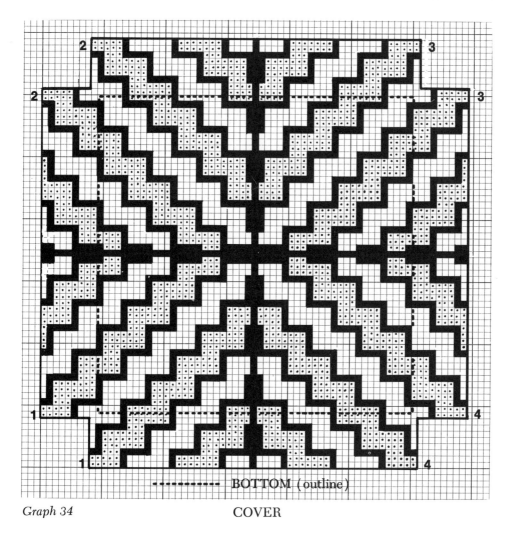

Graph 34   COVER

6. To assemble, fold the corners of the cover so that the points of each corner come together (indicated by numbers on the graph), and bind stitch in gray. Join all four sides with gray binding stitch. Attach the bottom in the same manner. Use binding stitch along the edges of the box and also the edges of the cover. See Plate 12.

SCISSORS CASE

MATERIALS

One sheet of 7-mesh Fashion Ease plastic canvas, 11 by 14 inches
Persian yarn (approx.):

> 10 yards of orange
> 10 yards of gray
> 8 yards of peach

Tapestry needle, size 18
Lightweight gray fabric, 5 by 11 inches (optional)

INSTRUCTIONS

1. The scissors case consists of two panels, front and back. Before beginning to embroider the back part, locate and cut out the small area for hanging (see graph). Put a binding stitch, in gray, around the opening.

2. Embroider the gray areas of both pieces in cross-stitch with a single strand.

3. Follow the graph and fill in the areas between the gray in Byzantine stitch with double-strand yarn, alternately using orange and peach. Note that the back part does not need to be embroidered all the way down.

4. Cut out both parts, leaving one ridge all around. Use a binding stitch, single strand, for the upper area of the back panel, around the top edge of the front panel, and down the two sides to 1 inch. This forms a lip that is not attached to the back panel.

5. Now lay the front panel over the back panel so that the pattern matches. Join the two layers on both sides, also using a binding stitch (excluding the lip). The front part is purposely cut larger so that it curves slightly outward to create sufficient space for the scissors to be stored with ease.

6. When bind stitching the bottom, stitch twice into the extra hole at each end of the back panel to compensate for the narrowness. The bottom, too, will curve slightly. See Plate 12.

7. *Optional:* Line the back of the case by cutting the fabric the same size as the case, then tuck under ⅛ inch, and slip stitch.

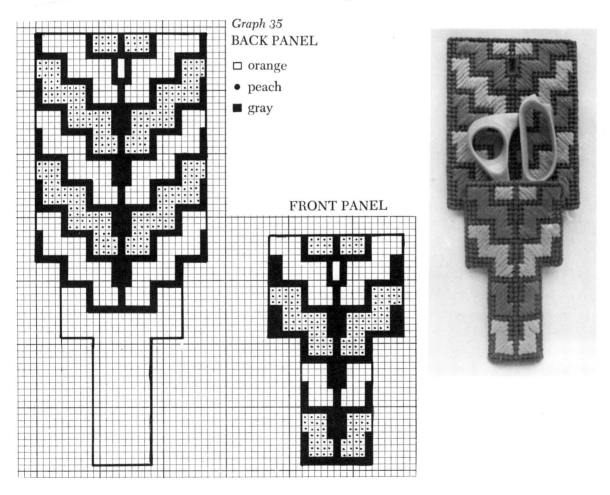

Graph 35
BACK PANEL

□ orange

• peach

■ gray

FRONT PANEL

PINCUSHION

MATERIALS

Four squares of 7-mesh Fashion Ease plastic canvas, 3 by 3 inches each
Persian yarn (approx.):

    16 yards of orange
    16 yards of gray
    12 yards of peach

Tapestry needle, size 18
Polyester fiber fill

INSTRUCTIONS

1. Cut two of the squares into halves, thus eliminating the center ridges. These four panels are the sides of the pincushion. The two other squares become the bottom and the top.

2. Embroider all six parts by first working the gray areas, then the peach, in cross-stitch with single-strand thread. Fill in the orange areas in Byzantine stitch using double-strand yarn (see graph).

3. Join the four sides with a binding stitch in single-strand gray yarn; next attach the bottom in the same manner.

4. Bind stitch one edge of the top to the cushion, stuff with polyester fill, and finish the other three edges.

5. Onto each upper corner attach a small tassel made with a strand of the

Graph 36

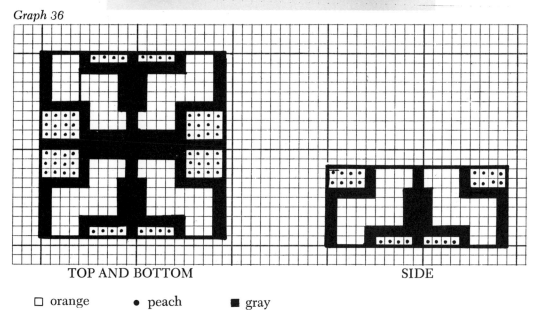

TOP AND BOTTOM   SIDE

☐ orange   ● peach   ■ gray

gray yarn (see page 126 for directions on how to make a tassel). See
Plate 12.

6. If you wish to hang the pincushion, sew a small loop to a bottom corner.

TRINKET BOX

MATERIALS

Six squares of 7-mesh Fashion Ease plastic canvas, 3 by 3 inches each
Persian yarn (approx.):
    24 yards of orange
    20 yards of gray
    18 yards of peach
Tapestry needle, size 18
One gray wooden bead or round button
Fabric in a coordinating color, 6 by 9 inches (optional)

INSTRUCTIONS

1. Embroider all six squares as indicated in the graph for the pincushion, page 93. Begin with gray and establish the design in cross-stitch. Next, fill in the area in peach, also using cross-stitch. The orange section requires double-strand yarn in Byzantine stitch.

2. *Optional lining:* Cut fabric into six 3-inch squares, line each embroidered panel by folding the fabric ⅛ inch under, and slip stitch around.

3. Join the four sides together with binding stitch, using gray yarn; then attach bottom.

4. Sew cover to only the top edge of one side of the box in binding stitch. Continue binding stitch around top edges of the box as well as along the cover.

5. Sew bead or button to the center of the top of the front square. Make a loop and secure to the center of the cover. See Plate 12.

·5·

GIFTS
TO GIVE
OR KEEP

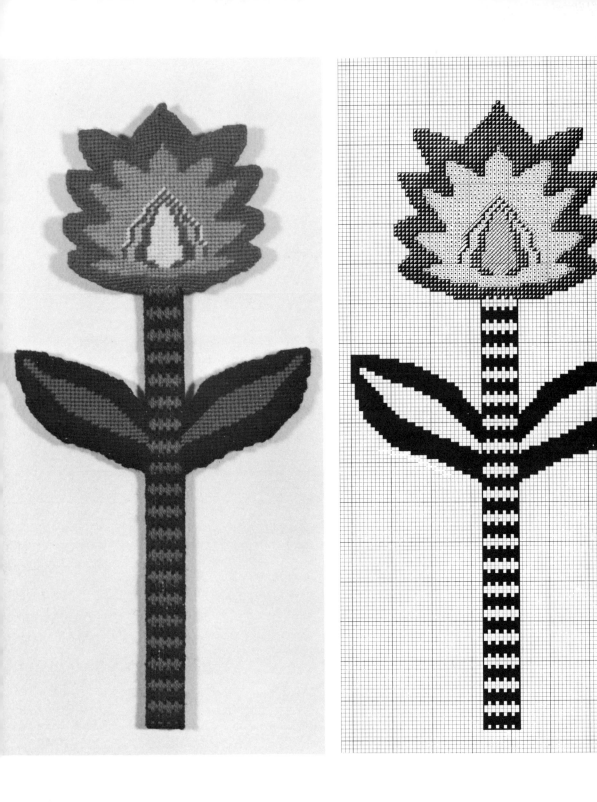

POTTED FLOWERS

FLOWER I: LILY

MATERIALS

Two pieces of 10-mesh Vexar plastic canvas, 8 by 16 inches each
Persian yarn (approx.):
     1 ounce of orange
     ¾ ounce of dark green
     ½ ounce of peach
     ½ ounce of bright green
     Several yards of white
Tapestry needle, size 20
One wooden dowel, ¼ inch in diameter, 16 inches long
Polyester fiber fill, for stuffing

INSTRUCTIONS

1. Establish the shape of the blossom by outlining it with orange yarn in continental stitch (see graph). Then fill in the indicated areas in orange, peach, and white, also in continental stitch.

2. Make the stem in Parisian stitch, alternating rows of bright green and dark green.

Graph 37—opposite

◢ orange   • peach   ∕ white
■ dark green   □ bright green

3. After outlining the two leaves, embroider them in continental stitch. Leaves are dark green with the center portion in bright green.

4. Leave one ridge of canvas all around for overcasting; trim away excess.

5. Embroider the second piece of canvas exactly the same way as the first. Trim.

6. Hold the two embroidered pieces, wrong sides together, and join the blossom portion with an overcast stitch. Stuff it with polyester fiber fill. If necessary, use a pointed object to push the fill into small areas. With dark green yarn overcast the stem down to the leaves (stem is not stuffed). Overcast both leaves, then stuff. Finish the stem.

7. Insert the dowel up the stem into the blossom as far as possible. Cut away any part of the dowel that protrudes and sew up the bottom.

8. Fill a flower pot with sand or small pebbles; insert the flower. You now have an everlasting bloom. See Plate 14.

FLOWER II: IRIS

MATERIALS

Two pieces of 10-mesh Vexar plastic canvas, 8 by 16 inches each
Persian yarn (approx.):

$1\frac{1}{4}$ ounces of purple
$1\frac{1}{4}$ ounces of dark turquoise
$\frac{1}{2}$ ounce of dark gray
Several yards of plum and lavender

Tapestry needle, size 20
One wooden dowel, $\frac{1}{4}$ inch in diameter, 16 inches long
Polyester fiber fill, for stuffing

INSTRUCTIONS

The procedure for making the iris is exactly the same as that for the lily. The only exception is that the stem is embroidered in stem stitch, with alternate rows of gray and dark turquoise (see graph, page 100). See Plate 14.

Graph 38—page 100

■ plum (blossom)   ① purple
● rose   ② turquoise
/ turquoise   ■ gray (leaves)
\ gray

Graph 38

FLOWER III: SUNFLOWER

MATERIALS

Two pieces of 10-mesh Vexar plastic canvas, 8 by 16 inches each
Persian yarn (approx.):
　　　1 ounce of ocher
　　　1 ounce of olive green
　　$\frac{1}{2}$ ounce of yellow
　　$\frac{1}{2}$ ounce of brown
Tapestry needle, size 20
One wooden dowel, $\frac{1}{4}$ inch in diameter, 16 inches long
Polyester fiber fill, for stuffing

INSTRUCTIONS

Make the sunflower by following the instructions for the lily. One difference: outline the leaves in brown continental stitch; fill in with green leaf stitch. For stem make one row of leaf stitch all the way down; fill the rest with continental stitch in brown (see graph, page 102). See Plate 14.

Graph 39—page 102
① yellow
② ocher
③ olive green
■ brown

Graph 39

LIZZY (STAND-UP) DOLL

MATERIALS

Two pieces of 10-mesh Vexar plastic canvas, 20 by 14 inches each
Persian yarn (approx.):

> 2 ounces of skin tone
> 2 ounces of hot pink
> 1½ ounces of brown
> ½ ounce of white
> ½ ounce of light blue
> Several lengths of gray, purple, orange, blue, red, rose, and black

Tapestry needle, size 20
Two small white buttons
Polyester fiber fill, for stuffing

INSTRUCTIONS

1. One sheet of Vexar is for the front part of the doll, the other for the back.

   Front panel: Following the graph as a guide, outline the doll in continental stitch. Use the appropriate colors (skin tone for head, hands, and legs; hot pink for dress; gray for shoes). Fill in the design in continental stitch.

2. Embroider the pocket for the apron. Finish edges with overcasting. Note that the top of the pocket pushes outward when the sides and bottom are sewn onto the outline as indicated on the graph. This creates a usable pocket, perhaps for a small treat to be tucked in.

Graphs 40–41

① skin tone
② hot pink
B brown
○ white
v light blue
● gray
P purple
∕ orange
× blue
◢ red
c rose
■ black

Graph 40

APRON POCKET

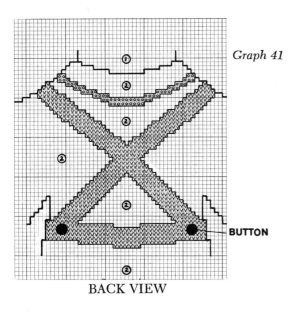

Graph 41

BUTTON

BACK VIEW

3. *Back panel:* Done in basically the same way. Instead of the apron, only the ties are indicated. Sew two small buttons on each end of the vertical tie (see graph).

4. Carefully cut out both panels, leaving one ridge of the canvas all around the embroidered areas. Then join them together by overcasting, naturally with matching colors. As each area is completed, stuff it with polyester fill. It is easiest to begin with the legs.

5. *Hair:* Cut brown wool into 10-inch strands. Join the strands by looping them together in the center with an additional strand of brown yarn. Instead of your fingers, a crochet hook can also be used for this task.

   Center the parted hair on the doll's head so that it covers the forehead and back of head. Fold the ends smoothly down the sides. Fasten the hair to the top of the head with occasional stitches. Pick up the ends and make a braid on each side, then tie with a piece of colored yarn. See Plate 15.

ADDITIONAL IDEA

If your doll will be admired only from the front, the back panel can be covered with a color-coordinated fabric instead of embroidered. In that case, it will only require half as much material and effort.

PHOTO ALBUM COVER

MATERIALS

Three pieces of 10-mesh Vexar plastic canvas: two pieces 11½ by 12 inches each, and one piece 2 by 11½ inches

Persian yarn (approx.):

    2½ ounces of rust

      1 ounce of orange

      1 ounce of yellow

    ½ ounce of moss green

Tapestry needle, size 20

Three pieces of rust-colored fabric for lining: one piece 26 by 11½ inches, and two pieces 3½ by 11½ inches each, for pockets

INSTRUCTIONS

1. *Front panel:* Begin on any outside edge of the cover and stitch the border in the following sequence:

   First row: basketweave, orange (four stitches vertically and three stitches horizontally; fill in four continental stitches in green on each side of the three horizontal basketweave stitches in order to achieve a straight edge on both sides)
   Second row: mosaic stitch, yellow
   Third row: brick stitch, green (compensate)
   Fourth row: brick stitch, orange
   Fifth row: brick stitch, yellow (compensate)
   Sixth row: continental stitch, rust
   Seventh row: as row 5

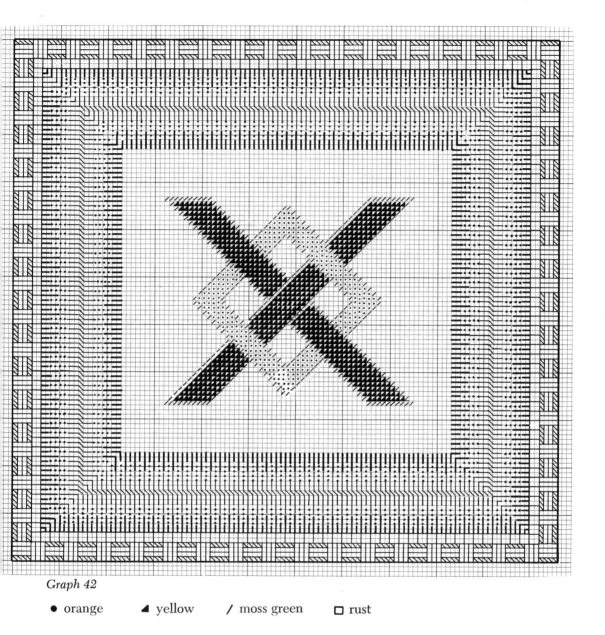

Graph 42

● orange   ◢ yellow   / moss green   ▢ rust

Eighth row: as row 4

Ninth row: as row 3

(See graph for complete pattern.) Trim edges to fit if necessary.

2. The remainder of the panel is embroidered in continental stitch. Locate the center of the front panel and stitch the center motif. Do the green

outline first, then fill in the design in yellow and orange. Stitch the background in rust. See graph for design of motif.

3. *Back panel:* Repeat the outside border of the front panel and fill in the center area in rust continental stitch (no motif).

4. *Spine:* Stitch the narrow panel in rust continental stitch.

5. Place the front and back panels on each side of the spine and join together with overcast stitching. Continue overcasting all around the edges of the cover.

6. Place the lining over the inside cover, tuck under, and slip stitch to the cover.

7. The following directions apply to each of the narrow lining panels: Hem one long side. Place panel over the lining of the cover so that the hemmed side faces inward. Stitch down the three outer edges to the cover to form a pocket. See Plate 16.

ADDITIONAL IDEA

Adjust the size of the cover for a telephone book or an address book.

STRAW BASKET

MATERIALS

One sheet of 7-mesh Fashion Ease plastic canvas, 11 by 14 inches
Swiss straw (approx.):
    4 hanks of dark green
    4 hanks of light green
    1 hank of medium brown
Tapestry needle, size 18

INSTRUCTIONS

1. Cut the sheet into six panels: two panels of the same size for sides; three panels of the same size for front, back, and bottom; and one strip for handle. See graph for measurements.

2. All panels are embroidered in kalem stitch with double strands of Swiss straw. Alternate dark green and light green for each kalem row on the front, back, bottom, and side panels. Stitch the handle in dark green only.

3. With brown Swiss straw, also double strand, join front, back, and side panels of the basket by using a binding stitch. Attach the bottom in the same manner.

4. Bind stitch the handle along the two long edges.

5. Locate the center of the front and back panels along the top. At these center points pin handle to the inside of the top edges. Bind stitch

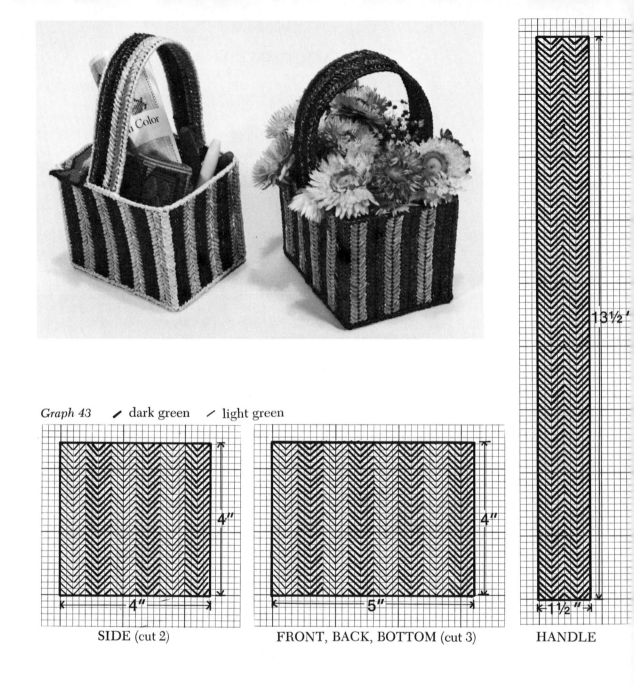

Graph 43   ╱ dark green   ╱ light green

SIDE (cut 2)   FRONT, BACK, BOTTOM (cut 3)   HANDLE

4"

4"

4"

5"

13½"

1½"

along the edges of the basket. However, push the handle strip down and attach by treating as one layer when bind stitching over that area.

6. Use the basket for utensils, fill with dried flowers, or put fresh ones in it by inserting a waterproof container. See Plate 17.

ALPHABET LETTERS

MATERIALS

One piece of 5-mesh Vexar plastic canvas, approx. 10 by 10 inches (size of
  canvas depends on the letter chosen; some require less)
Persian yarn (approx.): 1 ounce of the color of your choice
Tapestry needle, size 18
Small piece of fabric in the size of the letter, for lining (optional)

INSTRUCTIONS

1. Use double-strand yarn and embroider the letter in Rhodes stitch by
   following the graph. Note that each Rhodes stitch covers eight threads.

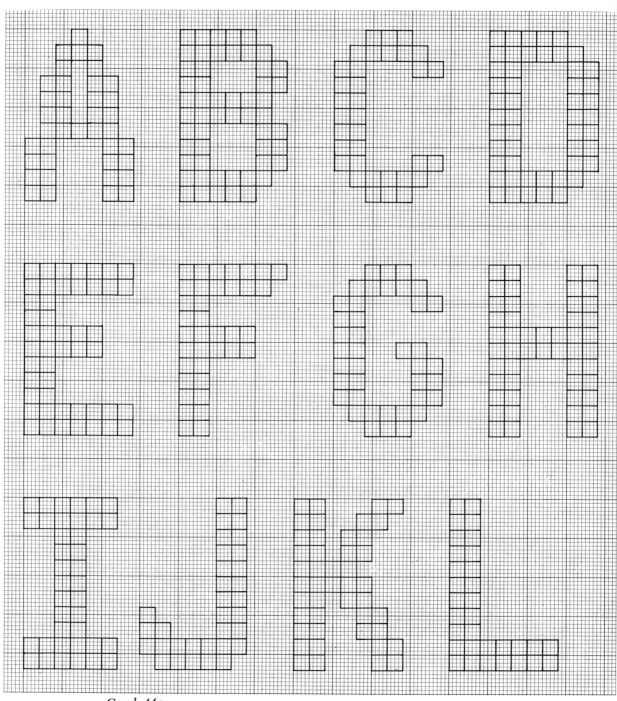

Graph 44a

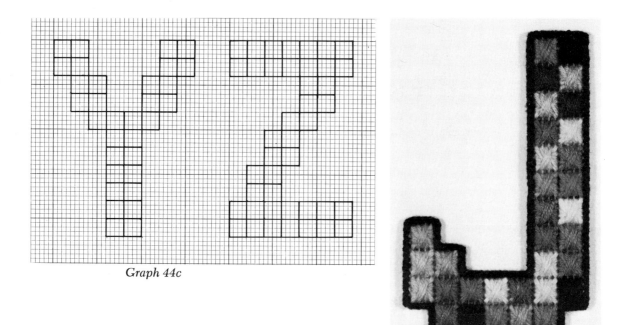

Graph 44c

Graphs 44 a, b, c   1 square = 1 Rhodes stitch

2. Cut out the embroidered area; be sure that one ridge is left all around. Finish the edges with a binding stitch, using either a contrasting color or the same color as that of the letter.

3. Line, if you wish, by cutting the fabric in the same shape as the letter. Tuck ⅛ inch under and slip stitch.

4. Hang on a cord, or apply double-sided self-sticking tape. See Plate 18.

ADDITIONAL IDEAS

Make each Rhodes stitch a different color and you have a calico letter. Or, using contrasting or complementary colors, complete the initials of a name to hang as a group.

EMBROIDERED ALPHABET SCULPTURES

MATERIALS

Two pieces of 5-mesh Vexar plastic canvas, 14 by 22 inches each
Persian yarn (depending on letter):

    4 ounces of yellow
    2 ounces of purple
    2 ounces of orange

Tapestry needle, size 18
Polyester fiber fill, for stuffing

INSTRUCTIONS

1. To create a design for each of these sculptured letters, use the graphs for the smaller versions. You must, however, count sixteen threads for each square instead of eight (see graph as an example). The following instructions are for a sculptured *A*. The same procedures can be adapted to the rest of the alphabet.

2. Each panel of the letter is embroidered in Rhodes stitch and double-strand yarn (remember that each stitch is worked over sixteen threads). Alternate the colors of each stitch in yellow and orange for one panel, and yellow and purple for the other side (see graph).

3. After both letters have been embroidered, cut them out, leaving one ridge. Join both with a binding stitch in double-strand yellow yarn.

Stuff the panels as they are sewn together. This will require less effort than stuffing the letter after the binding has been almost completed.

4. This letter can be hung, or it will stand up in the corner of a couch. See Plate 19.

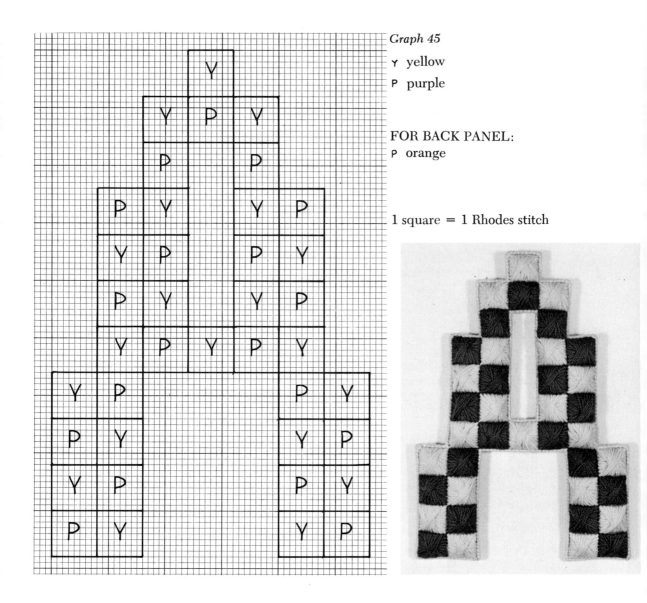

Graph 45

Y yellow
P purple

FOR BACK PANEL:
P orange

1 square = 1 Rhodes stitch

·6·

GLOSSARY OF
STITCHES
AND FINISHING
TECHNIQUES

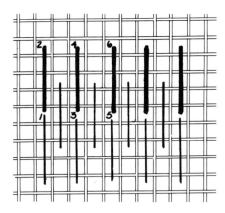

BRICK STITCH

This is a straight stitch carried over four threads and worked in horizontal rows. Stitch into every other hole in the first row, then place the stitches of the next row in between the stitches in the previous row.

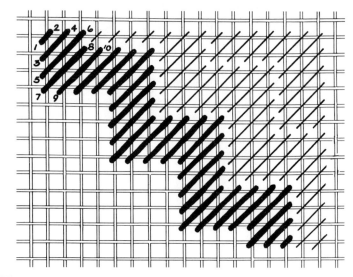

BYZANTINE STITCH

An easy zigzag stitch worked in a repeat of five horizontal and five vertical rows. For variety, place a row of continental or cross-stitch between each row of Byzantine.

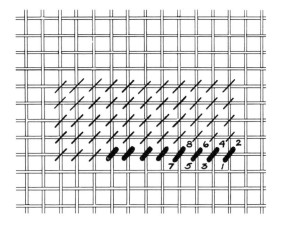

CONTINENTAL (TENT) STITCH

The most popular and versatile of canvas stitches. Each stitch covers an intersection. Begin at right side and work toward left, then at the end of row turn canvas upside down and stitch the next row again from right to left.

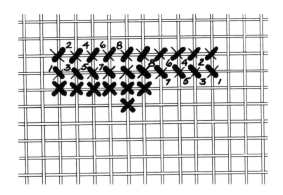

CROSS-STITCH

Two steps are required for the cross-stitch. The first stitch slants from lower left to upper right; the second crosses over the previous one and slants from lower right to upper left. The top stitches should all slant in the same direction.

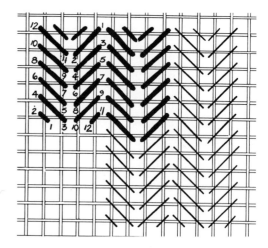

KALEM STITCH

Make the stitch over two intersections and work one row from the bottom upward and the next row downward. The stitch can also be worked in horizontal rows.

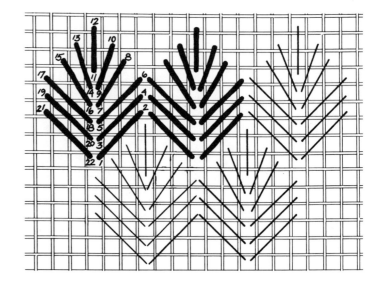

LEAF STITCH

Not as complicated as it may appear. Follow the numbers and begin on the right side, working from the bottom to the center top and down the left side.

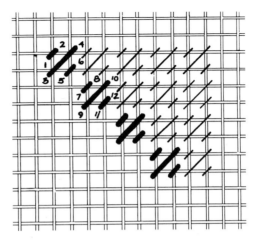

MOSAIC STITCH

This stitch is worked in diagonal rows and results in a square unit composed of three stitches: a slanted Gobelin in the center with a continental stitch on each side.

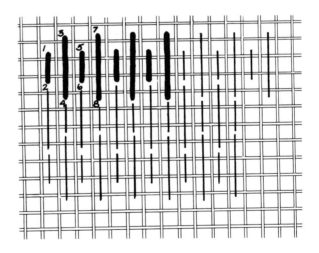

PARISIAN STITCH

A series of vertical stitches worked alternately over two and over four threads. For the second row, fit long stitches under the short ones, and the short stitches under the long ones of the previous row.

RHODES STITCH

Begin with a diagonal stitch from a corner to the opposite one of the square to be covered. Proceeding clockwise, continue stitching into each hole along the edges of the square until the area is completely covered. Because of the overlapping, the center will have a pyramid effect. The stitch can be worked over any number of even threads.

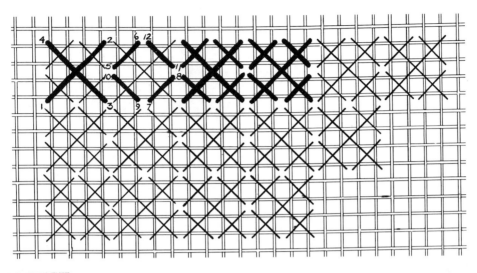

RICE STITCH

Start with a cross-stitch over a four-thread square. Add the tie-downs over each corner of the cross-stitch in a different color.

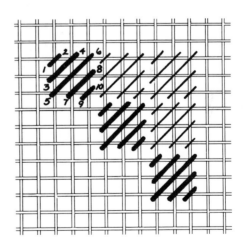

SCOTCH STITCH

This stitch can be worked over a three- or four-thread square, requiring five or seven stitches respectively. It is easiest to embroider in diagonal rows, but it also works well horizontally.

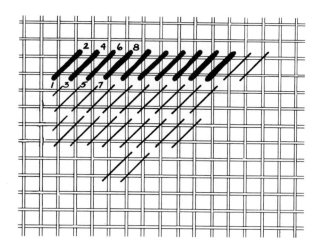

SLANTED GOBELIN

Stitched exactly like the continental, except that the thread covers two intersections with each stitch. It can be worked vertically or horizontally.

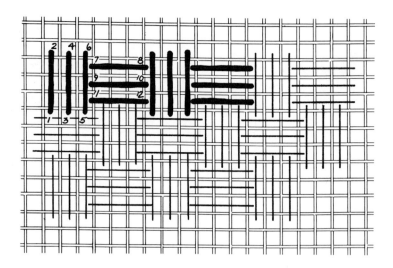

WICKER

A set of three vertical and three horizontal stitches makes up a unit of this pattern. It covers the canvas quickly and is very suitable for filling in a background.

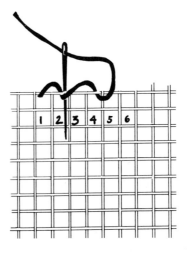

BINDING STITCH

All stitches are worked over the edge of the canvas from front to back. From hole 1 stitch into hole 2, bring yarn to hole 4, then back to 2. Repeat by stitching into hole 5, back to 3, then on to hole 6.

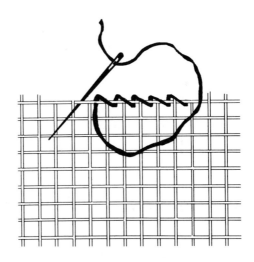

OVERCAST STITCH

Overcasting is a series of slanting stitches worked over the edge of the canvas. To assure complete coverage, stitch into corner holes three times. Overcast stitch can also be used to join two pieces of canvas together.

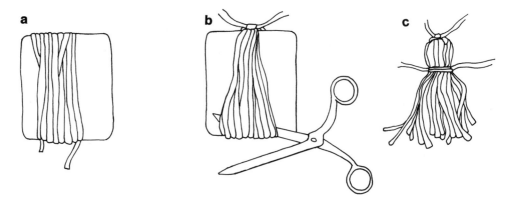

HOW TO MAKE A TASSEL

To make a 4-inch tassel, cut a piece of cardboard 4 inches square. Starting at the bottom, wrap the yarn around the cardboard until the desired thickness of the tassel is achieved. End the wrapping at the bottom (*a*). Take a piece of yarn and push it under the loops along the top edge of the cardboard. Tie it with a knot, but do not cut off the ends. Cut the loops along the bottom edge (*b*). About an inch below the top, wrap a piece of yarn several times around the tassel and push the ends of the yarn under the wrapped part (*c*). Sew the tassels to the rug or wall hanging from the loose ends of the tying.

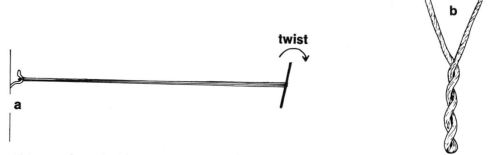

HOW TO MAKE A TWISTED CORD

The thickness of the cord is determined by the number of yarn lengths used. The length of the yarn should be about two and one-half times longer than the finished cord desired. Tie one end to any stationary hook and the other to a movable rod, such as a pencil. Tighten the yarn and twist the pencil until the cord folds on itself. Pull taut once more, fold in half, and allow to twist together. Tie a knot to keep from unraveling.

LIST OF SUPPLIERS

Should you have difficulty obtaining any of the supplies noted in this book from your local needlepoint store, write to the distributors or manufacturers listed below. A stamped, self-addressed envelope will speed up your request.

CANVAS

E. I. Du Pont de Nemours & Company
1007 Market Street
Wilmington, Delaware 19898

Columbia-Minerva
295 Fifth Avenue
New York, New York 10010

Tina of California
1156 North McCadden Place
Los Angeles, California 90038

YARNS

D.M.C. Corporation
107 Trumbull Street
Elizabeth, New Jersey 07206
Yarns, metallic threads, cotton perle

Paternayan Bros., Inc.
312 East 95th Street
New York, New York 10028
Persian yarns, rug yarns

RLL Enterprises
82 Manetto Hill Mall
Manetto Hill Road
Plainview, New York 11803
Rhodalure silver and gold

ACCESSORIES

Mail Order. Beads, buckles, bells, satin cords
Creative Fibers, Inc.
1028 East Juneau Avenue
Milwaukee, Wisconsin 53202
(Request up-to-date catalog)